SAINT BE

SAINT BENEDICT IN HIS TIME

RICHARD NEWMAN

THREE PEAKS PRESS
9 CROESONEN ROAD
ABERGAVENNY
MONMOUTHSHIRE
NP7 6AE · WALES · U.K.

Published in Great Britain 2013
Three Peaks Press
9 Croesonen Road
Abergavenny
Monmouthshire NP7 6AE
mail@p3p.org   http://p3p.org
© 2013 by the author

All rights reserved. No part of this publication may be reproduced, stored in a retrieval system, or transmitted in any form by any means except for brief quotation without the prior permission of the publisher.

The moral right of the author and artist has been asserted.

Designed & set in Joanna and Cambria
at Three Peaks Press

Printed in Wales
at Gwasg Dinefwr, Llandybie

A CIP record for this publication
is available from the British Library

ISBN 978−1−902093−18−5

Contents

Foreword	7
List of Illustrations by Peter Nash	8
Saint Benedict in his Time	9
Italy in Benedict's Lifetime	11
Arianism and Orthodoxy	15
Arian Beliefs and Practices	19
Benedict comes to Rome	23
Literary influences, Classical and Christian	29
Benedict departs from Rome	36
The Church Divided	38
Schism in Rome	40
Benedict and Doctrinal Disputes	47
Monks and Priests	53
Liturgical Continuities	54
Lay Leadership within the Church	58
The Monastic Household	63
The Monastery in the World	69
Conclusion	75
Note on the Author	80

In *Saint Benedict in His Time*, Richard Newman has written a fine little book that is weightier than it might at first appear. Newman's general thesis is that modern commentators on the *Rule of Benedict*, including some of the most serious ones, have more or less ignored the social and religious context of sixth century Italy in which Benedict lived and worked. To make up for this lacuna, Newman has read widely and deeply in the best current research on sixth century Italy and he makes this available to the average reader. He is not afraid to challenge some weak spots in the modern commentaries, such as my own downplaying of the abbot as a dominus, a master of a rural agricultural community.
I learned a great deal from this book!

TERRENCE KARDONG OSB
Editor, American Benedictine Review
Monk of Assumption Abbey

Richard Newman is to be congratulated on the serious, painstaking scholarship which shines through every sentence. We, the readers, (and I hope it will reach large numbers) should be grateful to be given in accessible and readable form this clear historical perspective. . . it makes a most valuable contribution to our understanding of Benedict.

ESTHER DE WAAL
Writer

Many thanks for the chance to see this. It's something that truly mirrors its title! Certainly, it is *not* a book *about* Benedict, but one that sets his life (or myth, depending on your position) in context, and illuminates many portions of the *Rule*. All in all, an excellent piece—it will be of immense value to Novice directors and directors of young monastics, not to mention Oblates.

ROBERT L. NIELSEN
Emeritus Professor of Philosophy, D'youville College Buffalo NY USA
Oblate of Portsmouth Abbey

I found the book highly readable, informative, and unusual—precisely in approaching the *Rule* through the history instead of vice versa. I shall certainly be recommending it to monasteries, and look forward to seeing it in print. It is refreshing to see an attempt being made, with careful but accessible scholarship, to read St Benedict in the context of his time, rather than simply within the text history of monastic rules.

MARK BARRETT OSB
Monk of Worth Abbey

Foreword

The aim of this book is to place the life of Saint Benedict into its historical context, and to describe the social and intellectual environment in which Benedict founded his community.

I hope it will complement the many excellent commentaries on Benedict's Rule for Monks and the stories about the saint in the *Dialogue* by Gregory the Great.

I have added numerous footnotes to my narrative in order to provide references to the English-language material for those who would like to explore the literature for themselves. I am well aware that some aspects of the subject can be taken much further than I have been able to do here.

I would like to thank the Bodleian Library of the University of Oxford for allowing me access to its excellent collections. I am also grateful to Mark Humphries and John Moorhead, who each made suggestions that were helpful to me in my research. Michael Woodward and an anonymous referee read the final draft and made valuable comments, as did my wife Sheila, who has been wonderfully supportive throughout. I would also like to thank Peter Nash for his linocut illustrations.

None of the above persons bears any responsibility for the scope of this book or its conclusions. If there are any errors or inadequacies in what I have written, the fault is mine alone.

Richard Newman
Feast of the Passing of St Benedict
March 2013

List of Illustrations
by Peter Nash

The road from Rome	Cover
The ravine at Subiaco	10
A family gathers for communion before a meal	27
Benedict ponders the Word of God	49
Monks gather for the Opus Dei	64
The Monastery at Monte Cassino	79

SAINT BENEDICT IN HIS TIME

THE FEW DETAILS we have about the life of Saint Benedict sit lightly on the history of his times. Most of what we know about Benedict comes from the second *Dialogue* of Gregory the Great, which is filled with stories of miracles and prophecy, but very few of the facts that we would normally expect in a biography and even fewer that link Benedict to the ideas and events of his time.[1]

Gregory's account has been analysed by many commentators and there is general agreement that the main purpose of the *Dialogue* is to inspire the reader with the example of Benedict's holiness. Indeed, some commentators have suggested that few of the details should be taken literally, or regarded as historically accurate.[2]

1. The version used here is T.G. Kardong, *The Life of Saint Benedict by Gregory the Great: Translation and Commentary* (Collegeville: Liturgical Press, 2009). References in brackets in the text are to this version and begin with D. The authoritative commentary by Adalbert de Vogüé is in A. de Vogüé, *The Life of St Benedict – Gregory the Great*, commentary by A. de Vogüé, translated by H. Costello and E. de Bhaldraithe (Petersham, Mass.: St Bede's Publications, 1993).
2. E.g. P. Cusack, *An Interpretation of the Second Dialogue of Gregory the Great: Hagiography and St Benedict* (Lewiston/Lampeter: Edwin Mellen Press, 1993), pp.151-52. This scepticism has been taken a stage further by Francis Clark, who has argued that the *Dialogue* was not even the work of Gregory, but of a Lateran official writing about fifty years later. See F. Clark, *The 'Gregorian' Dialogues and the Origins of Benedictine Monasticism* (Leiden: Brill, 2003).

Meanwhile, professional historians have given us a picture of Italian life in the fifth and sixth centuries in ever-increasing detail, a picture of social and political upheaval and of a Church that was struggling to resolve theological conflicts and establish a centralised administration. Very little of this contextual material has found its way into the commentaries either on the *Dialogue* or on Benedict's own Rule for Monks, the *Regula Benedicti* (hereafter RB). It is true that Benedict was writing a Rule of life for an enclosed community with spiritual goals and one would not expect him to comment much on the world outside, yet it is hard to believe that he was not influenced to some extent by the tide of events and ideas.

Italy in Benedict's Lifetime

BENEDICT WAS BORN about 480 C.E., the son of a gentry family in Nursia, in the Italian region of Umbria.[3] After a short period of education in Rome, followed by experiences as a hermit and as abbot of an unruly community of monks at Vicovaro, he successfully founded a cluster of small monasteries at Subiaco, near Rome. About 529, he took some of his monks to Monte Cassino, a prominent hill overlooking the road from Rome to Naples. There they constructed a new monastery, and it was there that Benedict wrote RB and lived until his death, probably in 547.

Benedict's life coincides almost exactly with the rule of Ostrogothic kings over the Italian peninsula.[4] The Roman

---

3. According to legend, Benedict was connected with the Anicii, a family at the pinnacle of the Roman aristocracy. This legend is discussed and dismissed by T.F. Lindsay, *St Benedict: His Life and Work* (London: Burns Oates, 1949), pp.16-18. If Benedict had been one of the Anicii, Gregory would probably have mentioned it, as it would have emphasised Benedict's humility in renouncing such an inheritance. It would also have been impossible to tell the story of the monk who resented Benedict as a social inferior (D 20.1-2). It seems more likely that Benedict's family was part of the provincial gentry, a lower stratum of elite society; see J. McCann, *Saint Benedict* (New York: Sheed and Ward, 1937), pp.39-45.

4. Some useful sources are J. Moorhead, *Theodoric in Italy* (Oxford: Clarendon, 1992); P. Amory, *People and Identity in Ostrogothic Italy, 489-554* (Cambridge University Press, 1997); S. Mitchell, *A History of the Later Roman Empire, A.D. 284- 641: The transformation of the ancient world* (Oxford: Blackwell, 2007); M. Maas ed., *The Cambridge Companion to the Age of Justinian* (Cambridge University Press, 2005); C. Wickham, *Framing the Early Middle Ages: Europe and the Mediterranean, 400-800* (Oxford University Press, 2005); G. Halsall, *Barbarian Migrations and the Roman West, 376-568* (Cambridge University Press, 2007); S. Barnish and F. Marazzi eds., *The Ostrogoths: from the migration period to the sixth century; an ethnographic perspective* (Woodbridge: Boydell, 2007); and J.J.

emperor had long since moved his capital to Constantinople, leaving a western emperor as viceroy in Rome itself. Gothic tribes had been moving into Italy from the Balkans during the fifth century, taking an increasingly important role in the army, and after a series of military coups, a Gothic military leader, Theodoric, became King of Italy and ruled from the northern capital of Ravenna until his death in 526.

Theodoric was an educated and cultured man and though his reign had some darker moments of murder and violence, he generally ruled Italy with great subtlety and respected many Roman traditions. The first half of Benedict's adult life therefore coincides with a period of stability and prosperity, a final flowering of Roman culture. After Theodoric's death the political situation deteriorated. Theodoric left no son to succeed him and the Ostrogothic court broke into factions.

The emperor Justinian, who had recently come to the throne in Constantinople, was determined to reunite the empire and found various pretexts to intervene in Italy. In 535 he sent an army to Sicily, which crossed to the mainland and, under the command of Belisarius, fought its way up to the north, finally capturing Ravenna in 540. The tide then turned, and the Goths under Totila fought their way back to the south. Rome was besieged in both campaigns and its citizens reduced to starvation. To make matters worse, Italy was swept by an epidemic of plague, which killed thousands with horrifying speed.[5]

In 552 a larger imperial army invaded Italy, this time from the north-east, so that Ravenna was quickly captured, the

O'Donnell, *The Ruin of the Roman Empire* (London: Profile, 2009), a book that wears its scholarship very lightly.
5. P. Horden, 'Mediterranean Plague in the Age of Justinian' in Maas, *Companion*, pp.134-60. The plague is thought to have been bubonic, though this is not absolutely certain. The epidemic was responsible for much of the mortality in Rome during the sieges and was blamed on the invaders from the East.

Goths defeated, and Totila killed. But success was short-lived. Over the next 50 years, successive waves of Lombard invaders poured into Italy and the country was reduced to turmoil. The last twenty years of Benedict's life – his years at Monte Cassino – were therefore a time of war, misery and upheaval.

Justinian and Belisarius may have expected a loyal welcome for the imperial troops but, in fact, the reaction of local people was mixed.[6] Naples resisted Belisarius's first push from the south in 536; Milan resisted the Goths when they counter-attacked in the north in 538; and the middling citizens of Ravenna – the small landowners, wealthy artisans and professional men – who had done well from serving the Gothic court, survived the short siege of the city in 540 and then adjusted smoothly to the arrival of the invaders.[7] Elsewhere in the north, Belisarius's subordinates made themselves so unpopular after taking control in 540 that the Goths were able to recover and fight on for another decade.

The Goths recruited Italo-Romans for garrison duty in the towns but they did not generally encourage them to join the Gothic field army, which was overwhelmingly Gothic in character and tradition. Indeed, the military functions of the Goths – their main contribution to Italian society generally over many decades – and the various administrative and financial arrangements used to support the soldiers and their families were key factors in the preservation of Gothic identity.[8] The Goths' religion – an Arian form of

6. Analysis of the campaigns can be found in P. Heather, *The Goths* (Oxford: Blackwell, 1996), pp. 259-76. See also P.A.B. Llewellyn, *Rome in the Dark Ages* (London: Faber, 1971), pp. 52-77. Both authors rely heavily on the contemporary accounts of the historian Procopius.
7. T.S. Brown, 'Everyday Life in Ravenna under Theodoric: An example of his 'tolerance' and 'prosperity'?' in [Anon, ed.] *Teoderico il grande e i goti d'Italia: atti del XIII Congresso internazionale di studi sull'alto Medioevo, Milano, 2-6 Novembre 1992* (Spoleto: Centro Italiano di Studi sull'alto Medioevo, 1993), v.1, p.97.
8. The relationship between the army and Gothic identity is very clearly explained by P. Heather, 'Gens and Regnum among the Ostrogoths' in H-W.

Christianity considered heretical by the Church – was also a distinguishing factor, but not the dominant one. It is not correct to say that the 'Gothic wars were also religious wars'.[9] There are no signs of the widespread friction between religious communities that would have provoked such a conflict and no signs of church burning or religious triumphalism in the aftermath of victory. On the contrary, there is much evidence of collaboration btween Catholic Romans and Arian Goths; members of the Roman elite, such as the writer and bureaucrat Cassiodorus, continued to serve the Gothic leaders long into the period of hostilities. As the military campaigns moved up and down the peninsula, 'most Italo-Romans swung with the wind'[10]— and wished that the gale would soon blow itself out.

Gregory's *Dialogue* links a few episodes in Benedict's life with the history of central Italy in the more turbulent period of Ostrogothic rule. We are told about famine in the countryside around the monastery and how Benedict gave provisions to the starving (D 28.1). Goths appear on various occasions: as an obedient monk (D 6.1-2), as a brutal landlord (D 31.1-3) and then as Totila himself, who came to meet Benedict, tried to play a trick on him and was appropriately humbled (D 14.1-15.2). Apart from this last story, which has a ring of truth and could have taken place in 542 or 543 when Totila advanced as far as Naples before turning back to lay siege to Rome, the Gothic identities mentioned in the *Dialogue* may have been invented

---

Goetz, J. Jarnut and W. Pohl eds., *Regna and Gentes: The Relationship between Late Antique and Early Modern Peoples and Kingdoms in the Transformation of the Roman World* (Leiden: Brill, 2000), pp.108-132. Heather also discusses the differences between himself and Amory (*People and Identity*), who sees the Goths as being much more completely assimilated into Italian society. Scholarly opinion generally favours Heather's position.

9. A. Bockmann, *Perspectives on the Rule of St Benedict: Expanding our Hearts in Christ* (Collegeville: Liturgical Press, 2005), p.2.

10. Heather, *Goths*, p.272.

in order to emphasise Benedict's holiness in his dealings with everyone, even the most apparently alien.[11] The Goths were a small minority of the Italian population. Their total numbers were probably no more than 100,000, concentrated in settlements in the north of the country and along parts of the Adriatic coast, with a small community in Rome and only the occasional garrison elsewhere.[12] Benedict's contacts with them and their Arian beliefs were probably very slight.

Arianism and Orthodoxy

THE ARIANISM OF THE GOTHS was a survival from the great religious controversy of the fourth century over the relationship between God the Father and God the Son. Most Christians considered that the matter had been settled by the Council of Nicaea (325), which declared that Father and Son were co-eternal and con-substantial, but Arians continued to insist that the Son, though still to some extent divine, was later and lesser than the Father and similar, rather than identical, in substance. A further council

11. The three Goths in Gregory's account also display different negative emotions: timidity, anger and malevolence. This perpetuates the Roman belief that barbarians were ruled by the passions, unlike Romans, whose lives were governed by rationality.
12. T.S. Burns, 'Calculating Ostrogothic Population', *Acta Antiqua Academiae Scientarum Hungaricae*, 26 (1978), pp.457-63. The numbers are much debated, but no modern authority would accept the old belief that Italy was swamped by Gothic hordes. Wickham, who is not in favour of the lowest estimates, is nevertheless able to conclude: 'There is no reason why the Gothic presence should have physically impinged on most Italians at all'. C. Wickham, *Early Medieval Italy: Central Power and Local Society, 400-1000* (London: Macmillan, 1981), pp.24-25.

of the Church, at Chalcedon in 451, had attempted to define the relationship of divinity and humanity in the person of Christ. Arian ideas had been largely confined to the fringes of the Christian world, chiefly to the Germanic tribes of the Danube basin, but when those tribes moved into the western Mediterranean and became the ruling power in North Africa, Spain, Gaul and Italy, Arianism once again became a challenge to orthodox belief.

It is thought that Benedict, when writing RB, took up the cudgels on behalf of orthodoxy. It is a striking fact that nowhere in RB can the name 'Jesus' be found; instead, Benedict always uses the words 'Christ', 'Lord' or 'King'. This is no coincidence. Benedict cuts short biblical quotations in order to exclude the name 'Jesus', [13] and downplays details of Jesus's ministry. It has been suggested that Benedict was trying to emphasise the divinity of Jesus as a counter to the Arianism of the Goths, who supposedly emphasised Jesus's humanity.[14]

If Benedict was indeed trying to assert Catholic orthodoxy against Arianism – that is, to assert the full divinity of Christ, united with full humanity in one person – a more obvious way of doing so would have been to use the two appellations of 'Jesus' and 'Christ' together on every occasion. We might also ask why, if Benedict was carrying out a campaign against Arianism, he did it through the medium of a monastic Rule which would have been read by only a small number of monks in monasteries. But leaving these points aside, it would seem that the impact on Benedict of the Goths and Arianism has been much exaggerated.

13. E.g. RB 2.20 from Gal 3:28 and RB 25.4 from 1 Cor 5:5.
14. M-G. Dubois, 'The Place of Christ in Benedictine Spirituality', Cistercian Studies, 24 (1989), p.109; A. Borias, 'Christ and the Monk', Monastic Studies, 10 (1974), p.116. Borias goes so far as to describe this as 'militant anti-Arianism', though he gives no evidence of a campaign on Benedict's part.

The religious policy of the Ostrogothic kings was tolerant and non-interventionist—quite the opposite of the Arian Vandal rulers in North Africa. Theodoric himself was an Arian, but there were Catholics in his immediate family, in his court and elsewhere in the Gothic community. He made it clear, early in his reign, that he would leave the Church to settle its own affairs and would protect its rights and property. This was the basis of the good relationship that normally existed between him and the Church leaders.

Pope Gelasius (492-96) referred to him as 'a most excellent man, my son King Theodoric',[15] and Pope Hormisdas (514-23) developed such a warm relationship with him that Theodoric was moved to present Hormisdas with two large silver candelabra for use in his church.[16] When Theodoric visited Rome in 500 he is said to have gone into St Peter's 'most devoutly and like a Catholic'.[17] It would be unfair to think that this was just a charade; he seems genuinely to have thought that religious belief was a personal matter and should be respected; he once told the Jews of Genoa: 'I cannot command your faith, for no one is forced to believe against his will'.[18]

Theodoric was proud of his Gothic religion and endowed it handsomely, but he refused to prevent the conversion of other Goths to Catholicism. Theodoric's own Arianism was therefore not an issue. The popes were much more likely to pin the label of 'heretic' on to the emperor in Constantinople

15. Quoted by Amory, *People and Identity*, p.200.
16. Such gifts were rare, presumably because they endangered Theodoric's policy of even-handedness between church factions. But after summoning bishop Caesarius of Arles in order to berate him for some of his activities, Theodoric sent him home with a gift and a large donation. 'I see the face of an angel', he told his courtiers. W. Klingshirn, *Caesarius of Arles: The Making of a Christian Community in Late Antique Gaul* (Cambridge University Press, 1994), pp.125-6.
17. Quoted by Moorhead, *Theodoric*, p.93.
18. Quoted by D.M. Deliyannis, *Ravenna in Late Antiquity* (Cambridge University Press, 2010), p.142.

than the king in Ravenna. For most of Benedict's lifetime the pope was at loggerheads with the emperor over the latter's meddling in ecclesiastical politics and his compromises with the monophysite theology that was popular in the East.

In the last years of his life, Theodoric's relationship with the Catholic Church became tetchy. Changes in the international situation made Theodoric feel beleaguered. New factions began to form in Rome and Ravenna. In Constantinople, Justinian began to attack the small Arian community there, closing churches and forcibly converting their congregations. Theodoric demolished a Catholic chapel outside Verona, apparently as a reprisal; he also ordered the trial and subsequent execution of the philosopher Boethius, which some have seen as an anti-Catholic move.[19] In 526 he sent the current pope, John I, on a mission to Constantinople to persuade Justinian to reverse his policies. John had reasons of his own for meeting Justinian, and in those respects his mission was a success, but he failed to secure all Theodoric's objectives and when he returned to

---

19. See J. Richards, *The Popes and the Papacy in the Early Middle Ages, 476-752* (London: Routledge and Kegan Paul, 1979), pp.110-13; Amory, *People and Identity*, pp.215-20; T.F.X. Noble, 'Theodoric and the Papacy', pp.419-22 and T.S. Brown, 'Everyday Life in Ravenna', pp.94-5 both in [Anon] *Teoderico il grande*. Relationships between the religious communities of Ravenna had been unusually tense, partly because Arians were so numerous in the city and partly because the Catholics were very pushy, having ambitions to raise their diocese to the status of a new patriarchate. Catholics had also rioted against the Jews of the city, burning their synagogues, and Theodoric had forced them to pay the Jews an indemnity. It was rumoured that Theodoric planned to order Arians to take over all Catholic churches in Italy, but such a move – even if it had been practicable – has not been corroborated by any contemporary sources. It may be this rumour that leads Bockmann, *Perspectives*, to say that Arianism 'was a real danger to the Catholic Church because of the rule of the Ostrogoths' (p.2). The events of Theodoric's final years are carefully analysed by Moorhead, *Theodoric*, pp.212-45. Most historians now attribute the fall of Boethius to factional struggles in which Boethius backed the wrong side.

Ravenna, Theodoric put him under house arrest, where John unfortunately died. This immediately gave rise to rumours of ill-treatment and John was hailed as a martyr; in fact, it is much more likely that the pope, who was already old and frail, was simply worn out by his long journey.

The forces behind these events were essentially political, not religious.[20] The outpouring of public grief that followed the death of John did not translate into a wave of anti-Arianism. The popes who served under the Ostrogothic kings, from Gelasius to Silverius (536-37), were all concerned far more with heresies like monophysitism and semi-Pelagianism than they were with Arianism. When Hormisdas discovered Manichaean cells in Rome he had the heretics' books gathered up and burnt in front of the Lateran, something he never did to the Arians. Indeed, throughout these years an Arian church remained open in Rome without giving offence to Catholics, even to someone as sternly orthodox as Gelasius. It was not until Vigilius became pope in 537, placed on his throne by Justinian's soldiers, that Arianism was offered as a justification for war on the Goths.

ARIAN BELIEFS AND PRACTICES

BENEDICT MIGHT, as an inquisitive young student, have visited the Arian church in Rome. He is unlikely to have seen anything that surprised him. Half a century

---

20. Richards, *Popes and the Papacy*, is particularly forthright: 'the religious connotation is humbug. There is no evidence of Arian-Catholic tension in Italy. The real problem was political.' (p.112). Richards goes a little too far; he forgets about the situation in Ravenna.

19

earlier, the Arian bishop Maximinus had visited an orthodox church in Milan and been astonished to discover that there was little difference between his liturgy and that of the local Catholics; they 'appear to give the same baptism, the same sacrament of the body and blood of Christ', he wrote, and they 'likewise honour the Apostles and Martyrs'.[21] The Arian church in Rome was dominated internally by a mosaic of Christ holding an open book and flanked by the twelve apostles, led by Peter and Paul, the two martyrs on whom Rome's primacy as a religious centre depended. The mosaics did not differ in design from orthodox iconography and they remained untouched when Gregory the Great rededicated the church in 592.[22] The same was true of the church of Sant' Apollinare Nuovo in Ravenna, founded by Theodoric, decorated during his reign, and intended as his court chapel—and therefore a building where, more than anywhere else, one might expect to find examples of 'Arian art', if such a thing existed. But two series of mosaics in the church, depicting the life and passion of Christ in ways that might have had Arian connotations, were left untouched when the church was renovated and rededicated after the Goths had left, showing that these depictions of Christ were perfectly acceptable to Catholics.[23]

21. Maximinus, *Opus Imperfectum*, 905, quoted by A. Urbano, 'Donation, Dedication and *Damnatio Memoriae*: The Catholic Reconciliation of Ravenna and the Church of Sant' Apollinare Nuovo', *Journal of Early Christian Studies*, 13 (2005), p.97, fn.71.
22. Urbano, 'Donation', pp.87-91. The church is now known as S. Agata dei Goti. The mosaics survived until 1598, when part of the building collapsed, but there are reliable drawings of them in church records. These are discussed in R.W. Mathisen, 'Ricimer's Church in Rome: How an Arian Barbarian Prospered in a Nicene World' in A. Cain and N. Lenski eds., *The Power of Religion in Late Antiquity* (Farnham: Ashgate, 2009), 307-25. Mathisen sees no distinctively Arian theology in the mosaics.
23. Much has been written about these mosaics; Urbano, 'Donation', pp.99-106 gives a good summary of the debate. The mosaics are said to represent the two natures of Christ, but it is not clear which nature should be seen in each series, or which theology lies behind them.

To share an iconography is not necessarily to interpret its theology in the same way. If the Goths did not accept the Catholic position on Christ's divinity, neither did they follow the sub-sect of Arianism that denied Christ's divinity altogether; indeed, there are some doubts as to whether the Goths were Arians at all, since they disliked the arguments about divine substance that had taken place at Nicaea.[24] Such issues, they said, were unscriptural. Scripture had made it clear, in their eyes, that the Father was the God of the Son and that Jesus himself had demonstrated this. 'The Goths assert that the Father is greater than the Son', wrote the early church historian Theodoret, 'but they refuse to describe the Son as a creature'.[25] They saw the Son as 'the only-begotten God', as a creator and mediator, 'a Son so great and so good, so powerful, so wise, so full' that it was right to glorify and adore him.[26] In practice, therefore, the significance of Jesus for the Goths may have meant that the underlying

---

Similar depictions of Christ can be found in orthodox churches of the same period. The supposed Arianism of the mosaics has been asserted by D. MacCulloch, *A History of Christianity: The First Three Thousand Years* (London: Allen Lane, 2009), p.321. For a contrary view, see Deliyannis, *Ravenna*, p.156; Urbano, 'Donation', pp.106-7; R.M. Jensen, *Face to Face: The Portrait of the Divine in Early Christianity* (Minneapolis: Fortress, 2004), pp.159-65; and B. Ward-Perkins, 'Where is the archaeology and iconography of Germanic Arianism?' in D.M. Gwynn and S. Bangert eds, *Religious Diversity in Late Antiquity* (Leiden: Brill, 2010), pp.265-89.
24. The origins of Gothic Christianity are described in P. Heather and J. Matthews, *The Goths in the Fourth Century* (Liverpool University Press, 1991), pp.137-141. See also M. Wiles, *Archetypal Heresy: Arianism through the centuries* (Oxford: Clarendon Press, 1996), pp.40-50.
25. Historia Ecclesiastica, IV, 37 quoted in J. Stevenson ed., *Creeds, Councils and Controversies: Documents Illustrating the History of the Church, A.D. 337-461* (London: SPCK, 1989), p.38.
26. Maximinus, in the debate between Augustine and Maximinus, 15.9; trans. R.J. Teske in J.E. Rotelle ed., *Arianism and other heresies* (Hyde Park, N.Y.: New York City Press, 1995), pp.205-6. See also R.P.C. Hanson, *The Search for the Christian Doctrine of God: The Arian Controversy 318-381* (Edinburgh: T.T. Clark, 1988) and D. Rankin, 'Arianism' in P.F. Esler ed., *The Early Christian World* (London: Routledge, 2000), v.2, pp.975-1001.

theological differences between them and Catholics may not have been difficult to gloss over, particularly if the liturgy of the Gothic churches offered no challenge to orthodoxy. The Goths' emphasis on scripture was another point of convergence with the Catholics. During Theodoric's reign, scholars were revising the text of the Gothic bible, moving towards a slightly less literal and more idiomatic translation from the original Greek. In the process some western ideas were borrowed from the Latin bible. As the Latin bible was also undergoing revision at the same time, it is not impossible that ideas also travelled in the opposite direction.[27]

It would seem that peaceful coexistence was really the norm in relations between the religious communities; 'in usual church practice and people's everyday religious lives, there can scarcely have been much to distinguish Arians from Catholics'.[28] Generally speaking, the Church and the papacy were not very much bothered by Gothic Arianism. It is difficult to see why Benedict should have been bothered by it either. He presumably had reservations about Arian theology, but to express these by avoiding the use of the name 'Jesus' in RB, insisting always on the use of 'Christ' alone, would not have addressed them or the way that Arian Christianity was practised at the time—even supposing that Benedict was sufficiently affronted by those practices to make a point of opposing them.

Although RB reached its final written form in the 540s, we should not necessarily expect the events of those years – such as Arianism or the campaign against the Goths – to be reflected in its pages. RB has an air of quiet authority which

---

27. M.J. Hunter, 'The Gothic Bible' in G.W.H. Lampe ed., *The Cambridge History of the Bible*, v.2 (Cambridge University Press, 1969), pp.338-62; Amory, *People and Identity*, pp.240-43.
28. K. Schaferdiek, 'Germanic and Celtic Christianities' in A. Casiday and F.W. Norris eds., *The Cambridge History of Christianity: vol.2, Constantine to c.600* (Cambridge University Press, 2007), p.57.

could only have come from a long period of reflection and experiment. It is a summing up of Benedict's whole monastic experience, including his difficult time at Vicovaro and his successful years at Subiaco. And Gregory's *Dialogue* also reminds us of the importance of Benedict's formative years as a young man.

BENEDICT COMES TO ROME

THE FIRST PAGE of the *Dialogue* tells us that the young Benedict was sent from his home to Rome for higher education (D 1). Provincial gentry normally sent their sons to the higher schools between the ages of 14 and 17, so Benedict would have arrived in Rome in the mid-490s.

The Rome of those days was a paradoxical mixture of vitality and decay. The population of the city had fallen from about 500,000 in 450 to, perhaps, as little as 100,000 by the time of Benedict's arrival and it would fall to less than 50,000 by the end of the Gothic wars.[29] Some of the major public sites were still in use; for example, after visiting St Peter's in 500, Theodoric went to the Forum to meet members of the senate. Games were still held in the Colosseum. Some other places, however, were sadly neglected, their walls collapsing, their rooms filled with

---

29. These figures are from R. Krautheimer, *Rome: Profile of a City, 312-1308* (Princeton University Press, 2000), p.65, but the middle figure is contested by other authors. The downward trend of population may even have been slightly reversed during the years of Ostrogothic peace.

rubbish. Others were systematically torn apart as their stone and marble were re-cycled to other buildings.

The great houses of the city's elite were less numerous than they had been. These were places of astonishing size and splendour; it was said that they were little towns within the city, with squares, fountains, places of worship and different kinds of baths, as well as hundreds of inhabitants and a daily stream of visitors. But some elite families had fallen on hard times; the political changes of the fifth century in western Europe and North Africa had altered the flow of wealth to Rome from its former provinces and cut the elite off from its overseas estates. Some families abandoned their Roman villas altogether and moved away, often to Constantinople, so that the once-fashionable eastern slopes inside the city walls were becoming depopulated. The most conspicuous new developments were taking place under papal auspices: the greatest of these, the enormous church of S. Maria Maggiore, had been built in the 440s, its Ionic columns and its mosaics showing Christ and the apostles dressed in togas a symptom of the way that classical traditions were being carried into a Christian future. The city's elite had gradually become involved in this process. From the 390s onwards, more than twenty churches had been built in various parts of the city, mainly with money donated by wealthy lay people and mainly in districts where the donors' families had always been powerful. The pope and his officials began to fret about the quantity of church property and religious and charitable activity that was influenced by the elite, and was not under centralised ecclesiastical control.[30]

30. F. Marazzi, 'Rome in Transition: Economic and Political Change in the Fourth and Fifth Centuries' in J. Smith ed., *Early Medieval Rome and the Christian West: Essays in Honour of Donald A. Bullough* (Leiden: Brill, 2000), pp. 21-41. See also Krautheimer, *Rome*; B. Ward-Perkins, *From Classical Antiquity to the Middle Ages: urban public building in northern and central Italy, A.D. 300-850* (Oxford University Press, 1984); B. Ward-Perkins, 'Old and New Rome Compared: The Rise of Constantinople' in L. Grig and G. Kelly eds., *Two Romes:*

Gregory tells us that Benedict had a 'liberal education'. Such an education had a well-defined content, which Gregory would have known, and we must therefore assume that his choice of words was deliberate and accurate. Liberal education consisted of the three verbal arts – grammar, dialectic and rhetoric – followed by the numerical arts of arithmetic, geometry, astronomy and music. The order of these studies might vary somewhat from school to school, but grammar was always the starting point.[31] The numerical arts always came last; in fact, Benedict may not have stayed in Rome long enough to grapple with them. The study of grammar involved the analysis of syllables and words, syntax and style, with the aim of learning how language should logically be understood. A word-by-word analysis of a text might also, in the hands of a skilful grammarian, introduce the student to history, geography and many other branches of general knowledge. The aim of dialectic was to develop logical reasoning and the numerical arts were supposed to promote abstract thought. In rhetoric, the student had to argue one side of a case – revolving around some problematic, even improbable, issue – using not only the conventions of oratory, but drawing on historical analogies, moral values, a sense of justice and the law, inspired still by the speeches

Rome and Constantinople in Late Antiquity (Oxford University Press, 2012), pp.53-78; P. Brown, Through the Eye of a Needle: Wealth, the Fall of Rome, and the Making of Christianity in the West, 350-550 A.D. (Princeton University Press, 2012), pp.455-62.
31. R. Browning, 'Education in the Roman Empire' in A. Cameron, B. Ward-Perkins and M. Whitby eds., Cambridge Ancient History, XIV, Late Antiquity, Empire and Successors, A.D. 425-600 (Cambridge University Press, 2000), pp.855-70; J. Moorhead, 'Cassiodorus and the Order of the Liberal Arts', Studies in Latin Literature and Roman History, 6 (1992), pp.505-13; Cassiodorus, Institutions of Divine and Secular Learning and On the Soul, trans. J.W. Halporn (Liverpool University Press, 2004), especially the very useful introduction by M. Vessey. Bishop Ennodius of Pavia, a near-contemporary of Benedict's, discussed the content of rhetoric in letters about the education of his nephews; see S.A.H. Kennell, Magnus Felix Ennodius: A Gentleman of the Church (Ann Arbor: University of Michigan Press, 2000), pp.50-62.

of Cicero, now 500 years in the past. Whatever the artificiality of the curriculum, it provided the bureaucracies of the time with a supply of 'shrewd and active minds'.[32]

As for Benedict's religious education, it can be assumed that he learnt the Bible at home in Nursia, but he cannot have had a programme of formal religious instruction in Rome. No such programme existed; the Church did not provide one, and nobody drew up a curriculum of that kind until Cassiodorus did so in the 560s.[33]

On the other hand, there can be no doubt that Benedict's curriculum was steeped in the ideas of pre-Christian – and therefore pagan – Latin writers. The works of Virgil and Cicero were foundational texts for the study of grammar and rhetoric respectively; Ovid, Horace, Livy and others were also studied by generations of students.[34] Valerius Maximus had written a compendium of patterns of behaviour, both virtuous and vicious, arranged under various headings, and this was often quoted in rhetorical debates. Varro had gathered together an encyclopaedic coverage of the knowledge of his day (1st century BC) and his books were quarried by later writers, including Augustine. Varro was a particular influence on Servius and Martianus Capella, two of the most important grammarians of the fifth century, whose books were circulating in Rome in Benedict's student days.

Writers in the old tradition were now reflecting in their works the more eclectic culture of the fifth century. Martianus, for example, imagined the liberal arts as

32. H. Marrou, *A History of Education in Antiquity*, trans. G.Lamb (New York: Sheed and Ward, 1956), p.288.
33. J.J. O'Donnell, *Cassiodorus* (Berkeley and Los Angeles: University of California Press, 1979), pp.179-85 and 206-13. Cassiodorus floated the idea of establishing Church schools to Pope Agapetus (535-6) and Agapetus set up a library in Rome, perhaps as a first stage in this project, but nothing more seems to have happened, possibly because of the war.
34. I. Schuster, *St Benedict and his Times* (St Louis: Herder, 1951), p.42 claims to find many references to classical writers in RB.

bridesmaids of Philology, who was about to rise to heaven to be married to Mercury, the God of Eloquence. This literary device allowed Martianus not only to describe each of the arts, but to argue that the human soul can rise from the body 'through the exercise of its intellect' and to depict the old Olympian gods as intermediaries between humanity and Jupiter, the father of all things and a 'sacred intellect'.[35] All of this was still a very long way from a Christian conception of salvation or the divine, but it was something that Christians might have seen as giving support to their beliefs.

In earlier days, many educated Romans would have been able to read Greek, but by the fifth century the knowledge of that language had declined very seriously in most parts of the Latin West.[36] It was still taught a little in cities like

35. S. Gersh, *Middle Platonism and Neoplatonism: the Latin Tradition* (Notre Dame: University of Notre Dame Press, 1986), v.2, pp.603 and 616; W.H. Stahl, *Martianus Capella and the Seven Liberal Arts* (New York: Columbia University Press, 1971), v.1, pp.83-9.
36. P. Langlois, 'Decline of Greek Language in the West', *New Catholic Encyclopedia* (Washington: Catholic University of America Press, 1967), v.6,

Rome and Milan, and used occasionally in aristocratic families with ties to the East, so it is not entirely impossible that Benedict had a smattering of it, though it is unlikely. Nevertheless, Greek ideas, now circulating in Latin translations, continued to be an essential part of the intellectual currency of the Roman world. Boethius, for example, was concerned to apply Aristotelian logic to Christian thought and had plans to translate the entire writings of Aristotle into Latin, showing that there was an appetite in Italy for literature of that kind.[37]

The need for communication between the Greek and Latin worlds was shown by the career of Dionysius Exiguus. He was a Scythian monk who had been invited to Rome by Pope Gelasius because of his exceptional fluency in both languages. His official task was to collect and edit the canon law produced over the centuries by the various councils of the Church, held in both East and West. Dionysius was also an extremely charismatic personality and in the cultured circles of Rome he must have made quite a splash; he displayed 'in his own deeds the righteousness about which he had read in the books of the Lord. He had great simplicity coupled with wisdom, humility coupled with learning [and among] other excellent qualities he had this unusual virtue, namely, not to despise taking part in conversations with the laity'.[38]

Years later, Benedict drew upon Dionysius's work when writing RB; many turns of phrase can be attributed to one of

---

pp.731-2; Marrou, History of Education, pp.260-63.
37. Of the many books on Boethius, the one that sets him most completely into the context of his times is H. Chadwick, *Boethius: the Consolations of Musi, Logic, Theology and Philosophy* (Oxford: Clarendon Press, 1981).
38. Cassiodorus, Senator, *An Introduction to Divine and Human Readings* trans. L.W. Jones (New York: Columbia University Press, 1946), p.122

Dionysius's writings.[39] Benedict would certainly have known Dionysius by reputation and although it is pure speculation to suggest that he met him or heard him speak, it is not altogether impossible, and it would have been natural, when Benedict was working on RB and seeking support for some of his ideas, to turn to the writings of a person he knew and admired. The character and lifestyle of Dionysius may even have been the example that encouraged Benedict to set out on a monastic life after his departure from Rome.

Literary influences, Classical and Christian

Throughout the fifth century, the most important corpus of Greek ideas was Neoplatonism, which was known through the writings of Plotinus, Porphyry and others.

Most people, like Augustine, probably encountered these ideas piecemeal, were attracted by some, and only later came to realise that others were difficult to square with Christian belief. Plotinus's concept of a transcendent God – the One, ineffable and prior to all things – had obvious appeal, as did his idea of the individual soul freeing itself from the body and rising to ultimate union with the One.

The problem, as Augustine realised, was to explain how the soul's progress could made be available to everyone.

39. See J. Chapman, *Benedict and the Sixth Century* (London: Sheed and Ward, 1929), pp. 37-56; A. Wathen, 'The *Regula Benedicti* C.73 and the *Vitas Patrum*', *Cistercian Studies*, 19 (1984), pp. 208-31.

This was the bone of his contention with the writings of Porphyry, Plotinus's pupil. For Augustine, the soul's progress was assured by the Word made flesh and the mediation of Christ. But Porphyry rejected the idea of the divinity of Christ, wrote many polemics against it, and continued to see value in some of the old pagan and magical practices, which he thought could be given an allegorical interpretation. In spite of these differences, Augustine had a deep and continuing respect for the 'Platonists', as he called them, for representing, more than any other thinkers, 'the closest approximation to our Christian position'.[40]

As pagan ideas were replaced by Christianity, classical authors were reassessed in the light of the new beliefs.[41] New perspectives on the classics came from the *cento*, a poem made up of a patchwork of phrases from a famous author reassembled to create a work with a new theme. An example of this was the *cento* written by Proba, an aristocratic Roman lady of the later fourth century, who pieced together verses from Virgil to form an epic in which the Creation and Fall, as described in Genesis, were contrasted with the main events in the life of Christ, as described in the Gospels. Proba took considerable liberties with her biblical template, some of them imaginative additions, as in her description of Mary protecting Jesus from the massacre of the innocents, and some of them outright distortions, as in her rewriting of the

---

40. *De civitate Dei*, viii, 9. For the influence of Neoplatonism on Augustine see R. Russell, 'The Role of Neoplatonism in St Augustine's *De Civitate Dei*' in H.J. Blumenthal and R.A. Markus eds., *Neoplatonism and Early Christian Thought: Essays in Honour of A.H. Armstrong* (London: Variorum, 1981), pp.160-70 and J.J. McEvoy, 'Neoplatonism and Christianity: Influence, Syncretism or Discernment?' in T. Finan and V. Twomey eds., *The Relationship between Neoplatonism and Christianity* (Blackrock: Four Courts, 1992), pp.155-69.

41. This was especially the case with Virgil. For example, his *Eclogue IV*, written about 40 BCE, declared that the 'Firstborn of the New Age is already on his way from high heaven down to earth'. Various Christian interpretations of this were current in Benedict's time; see W.V. Clausen, *A Commentary on Virgil, Eclogues* (Oxford: Clarendon Press, 1994), p.127.

Beatitudes to support Roman family values.[42] Nevertheless, Proba's work was widely circulated and much admired. It was soon adopted as a school text and came to be regarded as one of the 'apocryphal scriptures'.[43] It is easy to condemn the *cento* as bad poetry, bad theology and generally bad taste, but it must have required a close knowledge of the sources and no little skill in bending them to a new purpose. A competent grammarian would have unpicked Proba's lines, showing his students how to take an analytical approach to both the classical originals and the biblical model.

By Benedict's time there was a substantial body of original literature on Christian subjects in both poetry and prose. One of the earliest Christian poets was Paulinus of Nola, who was also responsible for establishing on his country estate one of the earliest ascetic communities in Italy. Paulinus wrote in a traditional style, but avoided the classical references to Olympian gods, drawing instead on characters from the Bible.

A more significant author was Sedulius, whose lengthy poem, the *Carmen Paschale*, written around 440, retold the story of the gospels with a special emphasis on the miracles of Christ.[44] Sedulius was writing for an audience that found the existing translations of the Bible rather plain, so he set out to entice his readers

---

42. J. Curran, 'Virgilizing Christianity in Late Antique Rome' in Grig and Kelly eds., *Two Romes*, p.338.
43. Isidore of Seville (c.570-636) quoted by J. Stevenson, *Women Latin Poets: language, gender and authority, from antiquity to the eighteenth century* (Oxford University Press, 2005), p.69.
44. C.P.E. Springer, *The Gospel as Epic in Late Antiquity: the Paschale Carmen of Sedulius* (Leiden: Brill, 1988). For two perceptive essays on the *Carmen* see R.P.H. Green, *Latin Epics of the New Testament: Juvencus, Sedulius and Arator* (Oxford University Press, 2006) and R.P.H. Green, 'Birth and Transfiguration: Some Gospel Episodes in Juvencus and Sedulius' in J.H.D. Scourfield and A. Chahoud eds., *Texts and Culture in Late Antiquity: inheritance, authority and change* (Swansea: Classical Press of Wales, 2007), pp.135-171. This paragraph relies on Green's analysis.

with a more consciously literary style. There are many echoes of Virgil[45] and much use of paradox and allegory. In his account of the Nativity, Sedulius stressed Christ's divinity – his radiance, his holding of heaven and earth through eternity – but also aspects of his humility—his taking the form of a slave (echoing Phil. 2:7) and his identity with shepherds and lambs. And Sedulius did not shrink from major theological issues: he asserted the perpetual virginity of Mary and plunged into the controversy over the nature of Christ. Sedulius's poem was enormously popular and influential. A new edition of it was prepared in Rome only a year or two before Benedict's arrival there, other poets began to quote from it and it was soon to be mentioned with 'conspicuous praise' in the *Decretum Gelasianum*'s list of recommended books.[46]

In his reflections on the scriptural text, Sedulius was only the latest in a long line of biblical commentators. By the end of the fifth century, these commentaries had themselves given rise to another literary form – the collection of extracts – and in Benedict's lifetime there was a number of these in circulation on the gospels, the psalms and the wisdom books of the Old Testament. Augustine towered above the other recent writers of Christian prose through the sheer quantity of his output, his range of interests and the quality of his thought and literary style. Within a year of his death he was hailed by the pope as one of the greatest of Christian teachers. Most of the theological debates of the fifth century were framed in terms that Augustine had set. Augustine himself was edited into collections of snippets, known as *florilegia*, or reproduced as extracts in the form of questions and answers to thorny

---

45. E.g. the 'two ways' of Matt. 7:13-14 are described in the same words as the tracks to Elysium and the Underworld in *Aeneid* 6:542-3.
46. In spite of its name, the *Decretum* was not by Gelasius. It was more likely to have been written during the pontificate of Hormidas.

biblical and doctrinal issues. It is very likely that Benedict first encountered Augustine's thought in this form rather than by reading the original works.

Benedict therefore found himself in a very eclectic intellectual environment during his student days, able to read Virgil and Cicero, Proba and Porphyry, the Bible and Augustine. It may be that this was reflected years later in the reasonable tone of RB and Benedict's advice to his monks to listen to juniors and strangers and be open to shafts of wisdom from unexpected quarters.[47] The young Benedict had learnt how to learn – 'learnedly ignorant and wisely uninstructed' was Gregory's assessment (D 1) – and this may have been the intellectual preparation he needed to write a Rule that was notable as a synthesis of monastic practice from different traditions.

The intellectual vitality of those days was not confined to the student population or the young. The families of the Roman elite had well-stocked libraries and a lifestyle that allowed them periods of reading and reflection on their country estates. They wrote histories and commentaries and edited the texts of classical authors; for example, Boethius's father-in-law, a senator and prominent figure in Theodoric's government, wrote a seven-volume history of Rome and edited a commentary on Cicero. Elite families also held literary salons at which friends would mull over the differences and similarities between pagan and Christian authors.[48] It was through activities such as these that the elite was able to 'drift into a respectable Christianity' while maintaining 'the secular traditions of the City of Rome'.[49] It was a situation that lasted long into the sixth century and

47. E.g. RB 61.4.
48. H. Kirkby, 'The Scholar and his Public' in M. Gibson ed., *Boethius: His Life, Thought and Influence* (Oxford: Blackwell, 1981), pp.51-2.
49. P. Brown, 'Aspects of the Christianization of the Roman Aristocracy', *Journal of Roman Studies*, 51 (1961), pp.1-11.

right through Benedict's lifetime, affecting the monastery through the contacts which Benedict had with aristocratic donors and the ideas which novices brought with them when they came to join the community. Some cultural events in Rome attracted a diverse audience. When the writer Arator completed his epic poem on the Acts of the Apostles in 544, the Church sponsored a public reading of it which was attended by clergy, members of the aristocracy and 'the people'.[50] The event was such a success that it had to be repeated three times.

Benedict gave the intellectual life of his monks a high priority. Over and over again in RB 48 he stresses the importance of reading. Monks were to have 'specified periods' for 'prayerful reading', and at other times they were allowed to read privately while resting on their beds. Seniors were to patrol the monastery to make sure that monks were not neglecting their reading or distracting others. On Sundays everyone was to study or read. In Lent each monk was to be given a book from the monastic library 'to read the whole of it straight through' (48.15); since books of the bible and commentaries were part of the staple fare for *lectio divina*, it is likely that this special book was something different, perhaps a theological work by one of the Church Fathers. A stylus and writing tablet were part of the kit distributed to every monk on joining the community (RB 55.19).[51]

These passages of RB have been overlooked by some historians. Some have taken the lack of a scriptorium at Monte Cassino as a sign of Benedict's lack of commitment to the intellectual life, but this is unfair; in the decade or so that

50. Kirkby, 'The Scholar', p.52, quoting a contemporary source.
51. Benedict's monastery must also have had a supply of educational materials for novices who joined as boys. Proba's *cento* may have been among them; it was commonly found in monastic libraries in the Middle Ages in association with educational books.

elapsed between the move to the new site and the writing of RB it is likely that the community was preoccupied with the construction of buildings and the clearing of fields and gardens. Others have seen Benedict's emphasis on work as antithetical to study when, in fact, in the monastic routine the two activities can be complementary; work done in silence can be a fertile time of reflection on what has been read. Some have claimed that Benedict 'confined' his monks to a narrow range of reading from scripture, the Church Fathers and discussions of monastic life (RB 73). But RB 73 was hardly the place for a full academic bibliography; in any case, the essential point of that chapter is that RB is only a beginning for the zealous monk, which applies as much to the reading list as to anything else. Furthermore, if a careful reading of the Church Fathers involved, for example, a reading of Augustine – as it surely would have done – the intellectual horizons of the monks might have been very wide indeed.[52]

52. J.G. Clark, *The Benedictines in the Middle Ages* (Woodbridge: Boydell, 2011), p.195 says Benedict 'confined' his monks to the books listed in RB 73, but on the next page makes the point about the breadth of material in the Church Fathers. A. Petrucci, *Writers and Readers in Medieval Italy: Studies in the History of a Written Culture* (Yale University Press, 1995), p.34 depicts Benedict as an anti-intellectual by (a) taking a very narrow view of the texts mentioned in RB 73, (b) ignoring RB 48 (c) brushing aside RB 55.19 as a contradiction that Benedict somehow did not notice, and (d) concentrating on RB 33.3, which he interprets as a threat to confiscate books and writing materials. In fact, RB 33 is a warning against the creeping privatisation of monastic property and books and writing materials were taken as examples precisely because everyone wanted to use them.

BENEDICT DEPARTS FROM ROME

BENEDICT GAVE UP HIS STUDIES quite suddenly, left Rome, and went in search of monastic solitude in the countryside.

Gregory explains that Benedict 'saw that some of his classmates were plunging into vice... [and] was afraid that worldly knowledge might cause him to fall into the depth of hell.' (D 1) We can well believe that Benedict would have shrunk from a life of tight wine-skins and loose women. But Gregory makes Benedict's change of course too radical to be entirely convincing. Would he really have thrown up his education and future career because of his classmates' behaviour? Students do, after all, have a choice about whether to go to the library or the pub, and can usually find ways of avoiding company they do not wish to keep.

Gregory does not describe the moral processes that led to Benedict's decision, even though he spends many pages of the *Dialogue* describing Benedict's later spiritual development. It would seem more natural for a provincial boy who recoiled from the life of a metropolis to go back to his parents. Instead Benedict went suddenly into a kind of exile at Enfide (Affile), a small town 50 kms to the east. Gregory tells us, rather confusingly, that Benedict 'sought to please God alone [and] went looking for a monastic habit' (D 1). If he had wanted to be alone with God as a hermit, he could have gone straight to the mountains; if he had wanted to become a monk, he could have stayed in Rome, where there were monasteries with a range of ascetic charisms to choose from. Instead he went to Enfide, taking with him the 'nurse' who had been looking after his household in Rome. We may infer from the presence of the nurse that Benedict had not severed his family links, and that these links may even have smoothed his path to Enfide, since we are told (D 1.1) that he was welcomed by the 'fine men' who managed the church of St Peter in the town. Gregory's account gives the impression that Benedict left Rome without a settled purpose and that it was really at Enfide, rather than in Rome, that he decided to turn his back on society and embark on a life of asceticism.

The time-scale for these events is uncertain. If Benedict had failed to settle into his Roman lodgings or his course of studies, he probably would have returned fairly quickly to his parents, as unhappy freshmen tend to do. The fact that he went instead to Enfide suggests that by that time Benedict was older and more independent. In Enfide he stayed long enough to acquire a reputation as a miracle-worker and then for this to become an embarrassment (D 1.2). We might, therefore, assume that Benedict's time in Rome should be measured in years rather than months, and his time in Enfide in months rather than days.

Gregory's account of Benedict's sudden departure from Rome is unconvincing in various ways. There is, it must be said, a suspicion that the story of the dissolute students is no more than a hagiographer's device for glossing over something in his subject's career that was difficult and embarrassing to explain. Was there anything going on in Rome at the time which might have had a sudden impact on a serious young man, and made it necessary for him to leave the city quickly? Indeed there was.

The Church Divided

The Church in Rome was in the grip of a double schism: a conflict with the provinces of the East over theology, and strife in Rome itself over rival candidates for the papacy. The theological conflict was more than a century old. Its main protagonists were the theological schools of Alexandria and Antioch with their different understandings of the nature of Christ. Alexandrian theologians tended to emphasise Christ's divinity, arguing that only a divine soul could be entirely free from sin and that therefore Jesus must have had a human body fused with a divine soul. To their critics, this left open the worrying possibility that if the human condition had not been fully experienced by Jesus, it had not been fully redeemed. The Antiochenes, on the other hand, emphasised the distinction between the divine and human natures that were 'conjoined' in the one person of Jesus; but if there was no essential union between the natures, it left open the possibility that the Jesus who hung upon the Cross was no more than an inspired man.[53]

---

53. The simplest introductions to this tortuous debate are D.N. Bell, *A Cloud of Witnesses: An Introduction to the Development of Christian Doctrine to A.D. 500* (Kalamazoo: Cistercian Publications, 2007), chs. 8-11 and P.T.R. Gray, 'The Legacy of Chalcedon: Christological Problems and their Significance' in Maas, *Companion*, pp. 215-38. For a more detailed discussion see W.H.C. Frend, *The Rise of the Monophysite Movement: chapters in the history of the Church in the fifth and sixth centuries* (Cambridge University Press, 1972); J. Meyendorff, *Christ in Eastern Christian Thought* (Crestwood: St Vladimir's Seminary Press, 1975). For the sequence of events see H. Chadwick, *The Early Church* (London: Penguin, 1993), ch. 14 and W.H.C. Frend, *The Early Church: From the beginnings to 461* (London: SCM Press, 1991), chs. 19 and 21.

Alexandrian theology was given a new depth and sophistication by Cyril, bishop of the city from 412 until his death in 444. Cyril argued that the Word became flesh as an act of grace, taking upon itself full human life, including a human soul and the capacity to suffer, without ceasing at the same time to be itself. Thus, God-in-the-flesh existed in a single subject with God-in-himself.[54] Cyril summed this up in a phrase that epitomised his theology: 'the one enfleshed nature of the Word of God'. However, parts of Cyril's argument remained obscure and his critics continued to complain that the human soul of Jesus had only a shadowy role in the Alexandrian analysis.

After another twenty years of bitter debate, the emperor convened a council of the Church at Chalcedon in 451. The council was presented with a theological summary by Pope Leo I, which the delegates proceeded to take apart, line by line, and test for orthodoxy against the writings of Cyril. The outcome, nevertheless, was a compromise between the 'one-nature' (or monophysite) position of many in the East and the concept of a union of two natures in Christ, which was favoured in Antioch and generally supported in Rome. The Chalcedonian formula said that Christ should be acknowledged 'in two natures' – a fateful phrase, which the monophysites rushed to denounce – while adding many qualifications emphasising the unity of Christ, which were drawn from Cyril's theology but which left the monophysites unsatisfied.

For Rome, the theology of Chalcedon became the new orthodoxy; for many in the East it was a great betrayal. When one of Cyril's successors as Bishop of Alexandria took a pro-Chalcedon position he was torn to pieces by a furious mob. Protest in other provinces of the East was vocifer-

---

54. J.A. McGuckin, *StCyril of Alexandria: the Christological controversy; its history, theology and texts* (Leiden: Brill, 1994), pp.182-222. See also 'First Letter of Cyril to Succensus', 6, trans. McGuckin in the same volume.

ous and often violent. The controversy became a seriously destabilising force in the eastern provinces of the empire.

In 482 the Emperor Zeno, far from secure on his throne in Constantinople, decided to look for a formula that would calm the monophysites while demonstrating his imperial role in doctrinal matters to the western parts of his empire. With the help of Acacius, the patriarch of Constantinople, he issued an edict known as the Henotikon.[55] This tilted the debate towards an Alexandrian position without going far enough to satisfy opinion in the East; at the same time it caused enormous offence in the West because of its theological compromises, its open criticism of Chalcedon and the autocratic way in which Zeno had proceeded. The whole controversy was enormously complicated by personal antipathies, rivalry between the patriarchs, and by the back-stairs diplomacy of Festus, leader of the majority pro-Eastern party in the Roman senate.

SCHISM IN ROME

IN ROME, POPE GELASIUS took a hard line against the Henotikon. His successor, Anastasius II (496-98) seemed more inclined to compromise—worryingly so, in the opinion of many clergy.

---

55. The text of the Henotikon, with a commentary, can be found in A. Grillmeier, *Christ in Christian Tradition* (London: Mowbray, 1975), v.2, pt.1, pp.247-56. Grillmeier says (p.255) that the Henotikon found a balance of some sort between different points of view, but 'still one cannot fail to recognise a weighting in favour of the Alexandrian monophysite christology.'

When Anastasius died, these differences manifested themselves in two rival popes, elected within a few hours of each other: Symmachus, a Sardinian, a recent convert to Catholicism and a deacon, was elected by the hardliners, while Laurentius, a priest from Rome itself, was the choice of the pro-Byzantine party.[56] It seems that Laurentius was heavily backed by Festus and the senatorial aristocracy, together with a number of senior priests in Rome; but the bulk of the clergy, anxious about the Henotikon, backed Symmachus. Theodoric was asked to adjudicate between the two and plumped for Symmachus, since he had been elected first, albeit by only a few hours. A synod of reconciliation followed a few months later, at which Symmachus was confirmed in office and Laurentius agreed to move to a bishopric in Campania.

That, however, was not the end of the matter. The pro-Byzantine party complained that Symmachus was selling off Church property to repay people for their support during his election; that he had celebrated Easter according to the Roman calendar, which differed from the Greek calendar of conventional usage by nearly a month; and that he was keeping company with disreputable women, in particular a lady named 'Conditaria' (Spicy). Theodoric ordered Symmachus to come to Ravenna and explain himself, but during the journey, at an overnight stop in Rimini, Symmachus saw a group of women from the Roman demi-monde parading along the beach—a demon-

---

56. There have been differing approaches to the story of the schism; see Chadwick, Boethius, pp. 30-46; Richards, Popes and the Papacy, pp. 69-99; Moorhead, Theodoric, pp. 114-35; P. Llewellyn, 'The Roman Clergy during the Laurentian Schism: A Preliminary Analysis', Ancient Society, 8 (1979), pp. 245-75; T.F.X. Noble, 'Theodoric and the Papacy' in [Anon] Teoderico, pp. 395-423; K. Sessa, The Formation of Papal Authority in Late Antique Italy; Roman Bishops and the Domestic Sphere, (New York: Cambridge University Press, 2012), pp. 212-46. A translation of the 'official' version of events is R. Davis, The Book of Pontiffs (Liber Pontificalis). Translated Texts for Historians (Liverpool University Press, 2000), pp. 43-6 and 97-9.

stration that had apparently been arranged on Theodoric's orders. Realising that his private life would come under further scrutiny, Symmachus abruptly returned to Rome, where he shut himself up in St Peter's.[57]

Theodoric now appointed a Visitor to run the See of Rome, Bishop Peter of Altinum, and told the Church's episcopate to meet and sort things out. These meetings dragged on through much of 502. Symmachus refused to cooperate as long as the Visitor was, in effect, usurping his position as pope, so the synod's enquiry got nowhere, yet Theodoric would not allow the bishops to give up and go home.[58] In the meantime, Festus and his friends brought Laurentius back to the city, where he occupied the papal offices in the Lateran. Supporters of the rival camps fought each other in the streets and much blood was shed. Eventually the members of the synod held up their hands in despair, acknowledged Symmachus as pope, and said they would leave his past actions to the judgement of God. While the synod met ineffectually, Symmachus had been busy: he ordained more than a dozen new priests to compensate for defections among his supporters and he spent considerable sums of money on charitable works for the city's poor.

When Symmachus himself called a synod at St Peter's in November 502 to celebrate his victory, it could be seen that most of the priests from churches in Rome were absent, as were many bishops from the dioceses nearby, but their

---

57. Only a few years earlier, Gelasius had enraged a large part of the Roman aristocracy by refusing to discipline a priest who had been caught in adultery. In making such a fuss over Conditaria, it may be that the elite was punishing Symmachus for the obstinacy of his predecessor.
58. W.T. Townsend, 'Councils held under Pope Symmachus', *Church History*, 6 (1937), pp. 233-59 has a useful account of the meetings and the reactions of Symmachus and Theodoric. There has been some doubt about the dating of the meetings; most historians now favour 502.

places were filled by younger priests and bishops from remote corners of the country, who were encouraged by noisy support from the plebs outside the cathedral. Symmachus took the opportunity to deliver a diatribe against lay interference in the business of the Church, couched in general terms but dealing particularly with the issue of Church property, on which he had reforms to announce. That seems to have been music to the ears of the bishops present, but it sounded a note of warning to priests of the churches in Rome, who were accustomed to working closely with lay patrons. This support in the city's churches enabled Laurentius to stay on in the Lateran.

Sporadic disorder continued in the streets until 506/7, when Theodoric ordered Festus to send Laurentius off to retirement on his country estate and ensure that all Roman churches were handed over to Symmachus.[59]

Benedict may have been at one of the higher schools in Rome when the schism broke out. It must be a possibility that he identified himself with the Laurentians and, like Laurentius himself, found it necessary to leave the city at the end of one of the phases of the schism.[60] Perhaps he took a

59. Laurentius died soon afterwards in straitened circumstances. He has gone down in history as an 'anti-pope', with all the obloquy that that entails, but he appears to have been a worthy candidate for the papacy and to have behaved with some dignity during the schism. Theodoric's actions may seem to have breached his own rule of non-interference in church affairs, but, in fact, they showed his 'delicacy in Catholic ecclesiastical matters' (Amory, *People and Identity*, p. 205). He tried, wherever possible, to leave responsibility with the bishops. When, in 506, he finally called a halt to the schism, he was prompted by fears that strife in Rome would combine with economic discontent and a deteriorating international situation (Chadwick, *Boethius*, p. 37).
60. The schism has been almost totally ignored by Benedict's biographers and commentators. Gregory would not have wanted to suggest to readers of the *Dialogue* that the saint might have opposed the election of one of his predecessors; it was better, therefore, to emphasise Benedict's disgust with worldliness, a conventional ingredient in hagiography. Among modern commentators, McCann recognises that the schism

principled stand on one of the issues in dispute and attracted hostility from members of the opposing faction. What is certain is that even if Benedict was not actively involved in the schism, or perhaps not even in Rome at the time, he would have known about the events of those years and the issues underlying them. The schism was symptomatic of controversies that reverberated through the Church for the whole of Benedict's lifetime and it is inconceivable that he did not have an opinion about them. Where might his sympathies have lain?

If Benedict had supported the Laurentians he would have found himself in the company of many devoted churchmen. Most of the priests who served the city's churches were in that camp. Dionysius Exiguus lent them some support, though he worked hard for a reconciliation and soon made his peace with Symmachus; so did a deacon John, almost certainly the John who became pope in 523. Some of the Laurentians had a reputation for asceticism, and if Benedict's character was already developing in that direction this might have been an additional reason for joining them, but it would be unwise to draw a general conclusion from this;

might have had an impact on Benedict, but shies away from discussing it: 'The experience would not edify him. No doubt he knew where truth and right lay and did not hesitate in his allegiance'; McCann, *Saint Benedict*, p.56. Schuster imagines Benedict in the crowd that greeted Theodoric outside St Peter's when the king made a state visit to Rome in 500, but says nothing about the schism; Schuster, *St Benedict*, p.22. Zelzer mentions the schism, but uses it to make a point about Gregory the Great; M. Zelzer, 'Gregory's *Life of Benedict*; Its Historico-Literary Field', *Cistercian Studies Quarterly*, 43 (2008), pp.335-6. Unfortunately there is a number of factual errors in Zelzer's account. Louis de Wohl, in his novel *Citadel of God* (London: Gollancz, 1960), pp.79-88 pictures Benedict in a procession escorting Symmachus to a synod when it is attacked by the Laurentians; Benedict then decides to withdraw from Rome because the city's factionalism 'opposes tranquillity of mind' (p.88). De Wohl may well be correct about Benedict's motives for withdrawal but, for reasons given below, it is unlikely that Benedict was ever in the Symmachan camp.

both factions contained men of all classes, outlooks and backgrounds.

Papal elections had been disputed in the past and Benedict would see them disputed again. However, the charges against Symmachus arose not from the election itself but from actions he had taken after he had been consecrated bishop. These threw a shadow over his reputation as head of the ecclesiastical household, a man who ought to be able to control his own body and manage the possessions of the household for the good of all.[61] Symmachus's charitable projects and property reforms were an attempt to rehabilitate himself in that respect. The main problem for Symmachus in 501-2 was the fact that he was suspended from office and was having to face judgement from his inferiors, a situation that undermined the concept of papal authority that successive popes had laboured to construct over the previous two centuries. Gelasius had restated this very forcefully: that Christ's commission to St Peter lived on in the Bishop of Rome, that papal discretion determined when synods should meet or their decisions be accepted and that Rome, and only Rome, 'may always judge the whole Church'.[62] Yet this was a very fragile dogma, challenged on every side. The emperor in Constantinople argued that as Christianity was the ideology of his empire, he should have a role in deciding doctrine. Eastern provinces of the Church called for more synods and meetings of the patriarchs. During the Three Chapters controversy that raged in the last years of Benedict's life, theological proposals came from many different quarters, even from a humble deacon of Carthage, all claiming to speak in the name of 'the universal church'.[63] Pope Vigilius, who struggled to contain the

---

61. Sessa, *Formation*, gives various examples of how the Bishop of Rome was seen as an ecclesiastical *paterfamilias*.
62. Gelasius, quoted by K. Morrison, *Tradition and Authority in the Western Church, 300-1140* (Princeton University Press, 1969), p.99.
63. C. Sotinel, 'Council, Emperor and Bishops: Authority and Orthodoxy in the Three Chapters Controversy' Article V in Sotinel, *Church and Society in*

controversy, found himself browbeaten by Justinian, manhandled by his soldiers, forced into ignominious retractions of his papal pronouncements and even excommunicated by groups of bishops in North Africa and Italy.

Church discipline was better in the West but very far from complete. 'It would', writes Peter Brown, 'be a serious anachronism to see the bishops of Rome as being, at this time, central to the Latin Churches of the West'.[64] The bishops of Arles and Vienne, for example, were preoccupied with competitive empire-building in Gaul; and it was normal, in the aftermath of one of the regional synods, for local bishops to enter upon a period of reflection before telling their clergy whether or not to accept all the synod's decisions.[65] By the end of the sixth century, the Church's decision-making structure was clearer and papal authority more secure. In Benedict's time, however, each pope had to struggle to defend − and if possible to enlarge − his authority over the Church and his control over its governance.

Late Antique Italy and Beyond (Farnham: Ashgate, 2010).
64. P. Brown, The Rise of Western Christendom: Triumph and Diversity, A.D. 200-1000 (Oxford: Blackwell, 2003), p.115.
65. It would therefore be anachronistic to assume, for example, that the entire Church instantly fell into line behind the decisions of the Council of Orange on semi-Pelagianism in 529. For the relevance of this to Benedict see T. Kardong, Benedict's Rule: A Translation and Commentary (Collegeville: Liturgical Press, 1996), pp.30-31. In any case, the decisions at Orange seem to have been somewhat less dogmatic than has previously been supposed; see C. Leyser, 'Semi-pelagianism' in A.D. Fitzgerald ed., Augustine through the Ages: An Encyclopedia (Grand Rapids: Eerdmanns, 1999), pp.761-66.

Benedict and Doctrinal Disputes

On the central theological issue of the schism – the differences between Rome and the churches in the East – Benedict is likely to have favoured a more open and conciliatory stance than that of the Symmachans. This is not to say that Benedict was a monophysite; rather, it is to say that he would not have wanted to cut himself off from the theology of the East. He might have wanted to see a continuation of the policy of Pope Anastasius, who seems to have been willing to listen to what the Easterners were actually saying, rather than attacking a distortion of their opinions, as Gelasius had done.

Benedict had an eclectic approach to theology and the Christian tradition. The pointers to this lie in Chapter 73 of RB.[66] There Benedict urges his monks to look beyond RB and draw inspiration from the writings of 'the Fathers': the Fathers of scripture, 'the holy catholic Fathers' – presumably those of the Western Latin church – and the monastic Fathers of the East. Benedict thought it desirable to wrestle with two rather different traditions – the western Catholic and the eastern monastic – and find a balance between them. He tried to strike another balance within the monastic tradition, urging his monks to read both Cassian and Basil, even though Cassian's emphasis on the eremitic life is not easy to reconcile with Basil's emphasis on the monastery as a community. Benedict clearly wanted his monks to hold the two approaches together in creative

---

66. There is a mass of commentary on Chapter 73. For a brief survey and a guide to further reading see T. Kardong, *Benedict's Rule*, pp.612-15.

47

tension. So Benedict's reaction to theological controversy would probably have been to continue a dialogue and try to discern the higher truth that lay beyond opposing points of view. Temperamentally, he belonged with the Laurentians.

The core of the theological dispute between Rome and the East was the relationship of divine and human in the person of Christ. In trying to clarify his own thoughts on this, it would have been natural for Benedict to have turned to the writings of a theologian he trusted, John Cassian. Benedict's admiration for Cassian is obvious in the way that Cassian's *Institutes* and *Conferences* are echoed in the pages of RB; it would therefore be astonishing if Benedict had not read Cassian's other major work, *De Incarnatione Domini contra Nestorium*.[67] Cassian wrote this in about 430 at the request of Pope Celestine to help in the formation of papal policy towards the mounting controversy in the East. In it, Cassian condemned schismatic theologians of both East and West and produced what he thought was a summary of orthodox belief. At many points, however, and in particular in his description of the single person of Christ, his language is in harmony with the voices from Alexandria. Cassian's main target was the same patriarch who was Cyril's most bitter opponent; Cassian wrote about the Virgin Mary in terms that Cyril was currently trying to promote; and Cassian repeatedly used the terminology of 'flesh' to describe the humanity of Christ, while insisting that 'the Son of Man

---

67. J. Cassian, *The Seven Books on the Incarnation of the Lord, against Nestorius* in *A Select Library of Nicene and Post-Nicene Fathers of the Church*, second series, vol. XI, *Sulpitius Severus, Vincent of Lerins, John Cassian*, trans. E.C.S. Gibson (Oxford and New York: James Parker/Christian Literature Co., 1894). The *Incarnation* has usually been condemned as second-rate theology, though that does not mean that Benedict did not read it. For two reappraisals which take a more favourable view of Cassian's Christology see D. Fairburn, *Grace and Christology in the Early Church* (Oxford University Press, 2003) and A. Casiday, *Tradition and Theology in St John Cassian* (Oxford University Press, 2007).

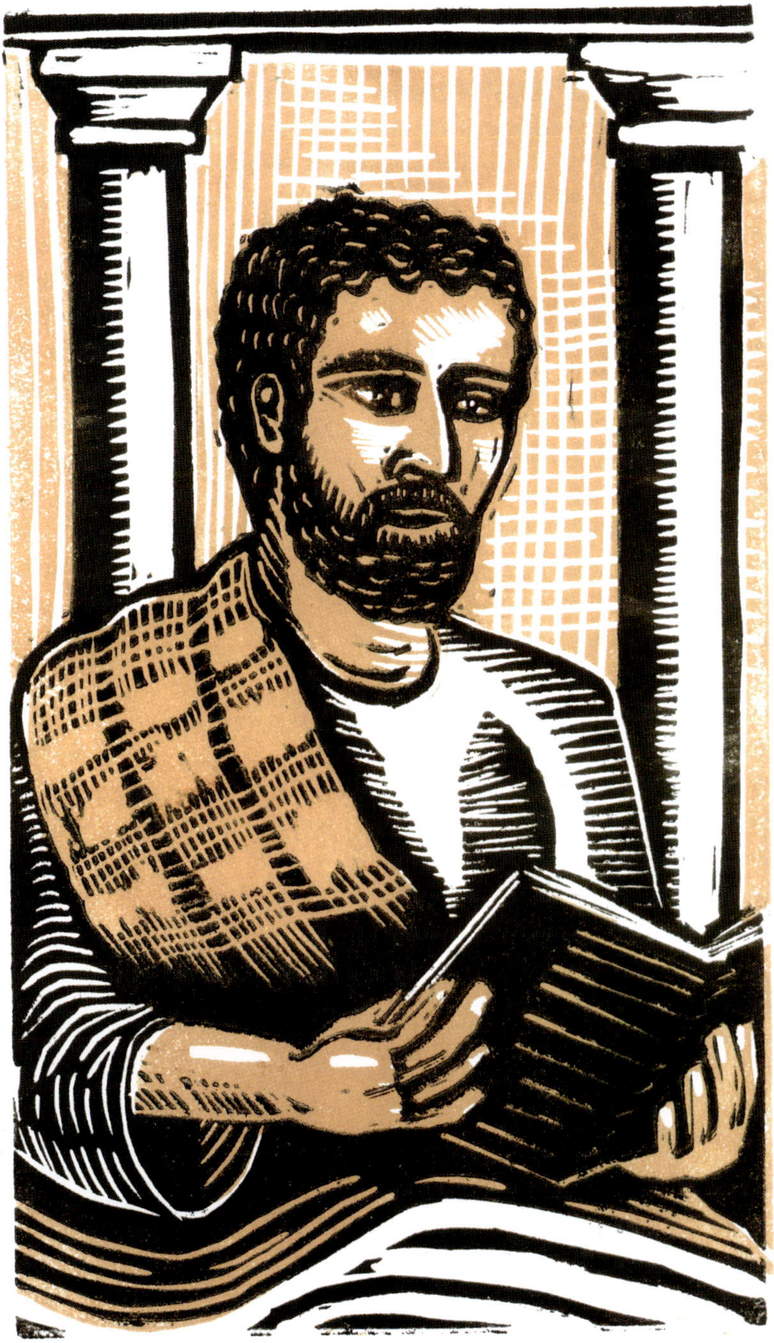

is the same Person as the Word of God'.[68] In arguing his case, Cassian largely ignored the events of Christ's earthly ministry, apart from the Passion and Resurrection—an approach which Benedict appears to have followed in RB. Benedict may also have noted Cassian's belief that 'truth always shines brighter when thoroughly ventilated, and . . . it is better that those who are wrong should be set right by discussion rather than condemned by severe censures',[69] a different stance from the frosty silence adopted by Symmachus in his relationship with Constantinople.

Cassian and Cyril took parallel positions on a number of points: for example, the action of God's grace and the distinction between Christ as the natural Son of God and humanity as adopted sons and daughters.[70] Cassian briefly discussed the belief that humanity, through sonship, could be partakers of the divine nature.[71] Cyril went much more deeply into that question, arguing that as 'the Only-begotten Word has become a partaker of flesh and blood . . . we have all become partakers of him, and have him in ourselves through the Spirit'.[72] For Christians in the East, this was a major step in the theology of divinization;[73] for Benedict, it may have given theological substance to the belief – fairly widespread at the time – that Christ was to be found in all the varieties of humanity, especially the poor and the sick (RB 53.15 and 36.1).

68. *Incarnation*, iv.6.
69. *Incarnation*, i.6. In spite of this, Cassian's tone may seem needlessly polemical to modern ears, which makes his tract rather tedious to read.
70. Fairburn, *Grace and Christology*, p.198 summarises these similarities at the end of a detailed analysis.
71. *Incarnation*, v.7 from Col.1: 12-20. See also 1 Peter 1:4.
72. *Commentary on John*, quoted by D.A. Keating, 'Divinization in Cyril: The Appropriation of Divine Life' in T.G. Weinandy and D.A. Keating eds., *The Theology of Cyril of Alexandria* (London: T & T Clark, 2003), p.151.
73. J. Meyendorff, 'Christ as Savior in the East' in B. McGinn and J. Meyenforff eds., *Christian Spirituality: Origins to the Twelfth Century* (New York: Crossroad, 1985), pp.231-51.

Cyril was very precise in the nomenclature he used in his writings: he referred to the incarnate Lord as 'Word' or 'Son' or else as 'Jesus' and 'Christ' written together. Very rarely did he use the name 'Jesus' on its own; on those occasions he was discussing aspects of the Word's human manifestation. Cyril condemned those theologians who argued that Jesus 'as a man' was merely a human invested with godly character. In his explanation of this point, Cyril said that 'the Only Begotten Word of God himself, as he becomes flesh, is called Christ'.[74] Whether consciously or not, Benedict followed Cyril's prescription exactly when writing RB.

When opinion in Rome was divided by the Henotikon and further inflamed by the Laurentian schism, it would have been natural to have looked again at Cyril's works and to have asked how it was possible – apparently – for Cyril to have been so influential in shaping the discussions at Chalcedon and yet to have inspired those very monophysites who attacked Chalcedon so furiously. Such questions do seem to have been asked; Dionysius Exiguus translated a number of Cyril's polemical writings into Latin, showing that there was a new interest in reading them. It is reasonable to suppose that Benedict was one of those who studied them anew.

None of this is to say that Benedict owed his views on these matters to Cassian or Cyril, still less to suggest that Benedict was a closet monophysite. Ideas about divinization were part of the theological currency of the time, even in the West; Hilary of Poitiers, for example, another student of Eastern thought, went some way down this route. Avoidance of the name 'Jesus' was also not uncommon; Sedulius, for example, uses it only twice in *Carmen Paschale*. The point

---

74. Anathematism 7 in 'Explanation of the Twelve Chapters', trans. McGuckin, St Cyril, p. 289. For Cyril's explanation of his use of 'Jesus' see 'Scholia on the Incarnation', translated in the same volume, pp. 296-7.

to be made here is that Benedict was likely to have seen enough common ground between his own developing ideas and the theology of the East to want to keep the lines of communication open. Not for him the inflexible stance of Gelasius or Symmachus.

Theological differences between East and West continued for the whole of Benedict's lifetime. The factional alignments of the Laurentian schism took years to fade away; Symmachus appointed so many priests and deacons – proportionately more than all the other popes combined between 492 and 526 – that he dictated the character of the church for the next generation and it was years before some of the Laurentians could be reconciled.[75]

Pope Hormisdas put the Henotikon to rest in 519 in negotiations with a new regime in Constantinople, but no sooner had he done so than a fresh controversy blew up from the East, known as Theopaschism, which was fortunately short-lived. There were bitterly contested papal elections in 530 and 532, and in 536 Pope Silverius was deposed by Justinian's army and replaced by Vigilius, who had been the least popular candidate in the previous election. In 544 Justinian made a further attempt to pacify the monophysites by getting the whole Church to condemn three theologians who had taken a particularly uncompromising position on the decisions made at Chalcedon. This controversy, the Three Chapters, raged for another decade.

---

75. Richards, *Popes and Papacy*, p.88; the statistics are also analysed by J. Moorhead, 'The Laurentian Schism: east and west in the Roman church', *Church History*, 47 (1978), pp.125-36.

Monks and Priests

Benedict would not have wanted to import any of the Church's theological disputes into his monastery. He tells his monks that if a priest asks to join the community 'do not agree too quickly' (RB 60.1).[76] Quite apart from the dangers of theological factionalism, Benedict wondered if priests would make good monks. He was trying to create a new kind of community, based on love and obedience to each member and to God. He was not creating an ecclesiastical elite for leadership and ministry, and he was afraid that priests who had been trained for such a role would expect to dominate a community of laymen.[77] Hence his wariness about the admission of clergy and his insistence that RB must stand above everyone—monks, priests and even the abbot. Benedict is surprisingly sharp in his warning against the danger of priests betraying the monastic ideal from within (RB 60.3).[78] He adds that

76. Quotations from RB are taken from T. Fry ed., RB 1980: The Rule of St Benedict in English (Collegeville: Liturgical Press, 1982).
77. Benedict may have been taking his cue from Cassian, who thought that the priesthood would draw monks away from contemplation into a vainglorious search for leadership within the Church; J. Cassian, *The Institutes*, trans. B. Ramsey (Mahwah: Newman Press, 2000), 11.14. The potential problem of monk-priests was well understood by Gregory the Great, who wrote: 'nobody can both do service to ecclesiastical obedience and persist also in the monastic rule in due manner.' Letter to John, Bishop of Ravenna, September 594, *Letters of Gregory the Great*, trans. J.R.C. Martyn (Toronto: Pontifical Institute of Medieval Studies, 2004), v.2, Book 5.1.
78. This seems to be the point of the biblical quotation in RB 60.3, which were Christ's words to Judas at the moment of betrayal. Some commentators have been unwilling to accept this conclusion, notably A. de Vogüé, *The Rule of Saint Benedict: A Doctrinal and Spiritual Commentary* (Kalamazoo: Cistercian Publications, 1983), p.292, who argues that Benedict was actually trying to introduce clergy into the monastery, 'though reticently'.

if priests are admitted to the monastery they should 'be allowed' (RB 60.4) to give blessings and say prayers, if the abbot agrees—a very grudging admission that priests might play a leading role. Benedict does not argue that priests are essential to the life of a monastery. RB's chapters on the subject (60 and 62) are highly conditional and imply that monasteries might well exist without priests as members; the chapters are quite different in tone from the imperative way that Benedict insists, for example, on the appointment of a cellarer or a porter. It cannot be said for certain that there were any priests at Monte Cassino in Benedict's lifetime.[79]

Liturgical Continuities

If the monastery did not contain any priests, it seems unlikely that there was a regular celebration of Mass at Monte Cassino.

The word *missa* appears seven times in RB but nowhere does it certainly refer to the Eucharistic rite;[80] indeed, the word was only just beginning to acquire that meaning, rather than its old meaning of 'prayers of dismissal',[81] and

---

79. For the reasons just given, Stewart is exaggerating when he says: 'We know that Benedict's monastery had priests among its members'; C. Stewart, 'Prayer among the Benedictines' in R. Hammerling ed., *A History of Prayer: the First to the Fifteenth Century* (Leiden: Brill, 2008), p. 218. We know only that, if priests were willing to live under RB and accept certain conditions, Benedict was prepared to admit them.
80. RB 17.4,5,8,10 in the liturgical chapters and 35.14, 38.2 and 60.4 outside. See the discussion by N. Mitchell, 'The Liturgical Code in the Rule of Benedict' in T. Fry ed., *RB 1980: The Rule of St Benedict in Latin and English, with Notes* (Collegeville: Liturgical Press, 1981), p. 411.
81. The earliest example of the new usage appears to be in Cassiodorus's commentary on the psalms, written in Constantinople in the 540s. See P.

Benedict may well have been unfamiliar with the change of use. Translators customarily write 'Mass' in RB 38.2, because *missa* closely follows the word *domenica* (Sunday).[82] However, the two words are in subordinate clauses of different sentences, both of which are in a chapter about the duties of the reader at mealtimes. Either Benedict has chosen an extraordinarily oblique way of referring to the Mass, or this is a very flimsy basis on which to conclude that Mass was celebrated each Sunday in his monastery.[83] Furthermore, Benedict makes no provision for Mass in the *horarium* of offices or the community's daily timetable. This omission is very striking when compared with Benedict's elaborate description of his Liturgy of the Hours, which even includes separate chapters on the celebration of Vigils and Lauds on Sundays (RB 11 and 12).

This is not to say that Benedict's community neglected the Eucharist. The word *communio* appears in RB in contexts that are consistent with the traditional sharing of communion outside the Mass. In the early Christian centuries, when there

---

Bradshaw, 'Mass' in *Encyclopedia of Early Christianity* (New York and London: Garland, 1997), v.2, pp.737-8.
82. Kardong, *Benedict's Rule*, p.314, is perfectly frank about the arbitrary nature of this translation.
83. The issue has been seriously confused by the great anxiety of some commentators to find precedents in RB for the daily conventual Mass, which became common in the Middle Ages and is now ubiquitous in Benedictine monasteries; see E. de Bhaldraithe, 'Daily Eucharist: The Need for an Early Church Paradigm', *American Benedictine Review*, 41 (1990), pp.378-440. A. de Vogüé, 'Problems of the Monastic Conventual Mass', *Downside Review*, 87 (1969), pp.327-38 agrees that there is 'not a word' in the liturgical chapters of RB about the conventual Mass and concludes: 'At most it is possible that [it] was celebrated on Sundays and feast days. But perhaps Mass was celebrated less often, even without fixed regularity.' (p.328). But in his *Rule of Saint Benedict* (1983), de Vogüé takes a more dogmatic position, translating *missas* in RB 38.2 as Mass, and concluding that 'Sunday Mass in the monastery oratory seems certain' (p.159). A more balanced view is taken by Mitchell, 'Liturgical Code', pp.410-12, which prefers de Vogüé's original conclusion.

were few churches and frequent persecutions, communion was necessarily a private affair in which families shared the sacrament before the main meal of each day, distributing consecrated bread that had been reserved from a recent Mass and taking a token sip of wine from a chalice they had blessed themselves.[84] From the fourth century onwards, when Christians were able to gather safely in large congregations, it became possible to receive the sacrament openly. The Church began to frown upon the widespread offering of the Eucharist in private places,[85] but only gradually developed the facilities to provide it in its own buildings; for instance, daily weekday Eucharist was not celebrated in Rome's basilicas until the sixth century, well into Benedict's lifetime. Private communion continued to be the norm for devout Christians – in the home and elsewhere – and reservation of the sacrament for this purpose continued unabated.[86] This seems to have been the practice in Monte Cassino.[87] RB suggests that communion took place after the prayers of dismissal at the end of Sext and before the main meal of the day (RB 38.2). Such a ceremony would have been completely in line with contemporary practice among the laity. The fact that Benedict says so little about it is further

---

84. K. Bowes, *Private Worship, Public Values and Religious Change in Late Antiquity* (Cambridge University Press, 2008), pp. 54-6; G. Dix, *A Detection of Aumbries with Other Notes on the History of Reservation* (London: Dacre Press, 1942), pp. 5-8.
85. W.H. Freestone, *The Sacrament Reserved: A Survey of the Practice of Reserving the Eucharist* (London: Mowbray, 1917), p. 28.
86. Dix says there 'seems even to have been an increase in the custom whereby Christians, clerics and laics, men and women alike, carried the sacrament with them wherever they went upon their daily business,' p. 22.
87. Benedict would have needed to get consecrated bread regularly from a bishop. It may be that the Bishop of Aquino, whose church was nearby, fulfilled this role. The bishop was said to have been a friend of Benedict; F. Cabrol, *Saint Benedict* (London: Burns Oates, 1934), p. 41. Benedict seems to have kept consecrated bread in his cell. According to the *Dialogue* (24.2), two monks went to Benedict's 'dwelling' to ask for a portion of the sacrament to place on a disturbed grave, and Benedict was able to give them some immediately.

confirmation of that fact; he would have thought it so normal that there was no need to labour the point in writing.

Benedict's monastic liturgy aimed at the goal that faithful Christians had always aspired to reach: unceasing prayer. A regime of seven daytime offices and a night-time vigil (RB 16), combined with periods of silence in between (RB 6.3, 38.5-6, 42.1), allowed the words of the psalms and readings from the Bible and the Desert Fathers to sink into the mind and inspire each monk to prayer and contemplation.

Benedict's liturgy was based on the psalter and the liturgy of the public basilicas of Rome;[88] but he added a fairly eclectic mixture of other features, most of them probably culled from the various migrant groups that had settled in Rome and were still worshipping there according to their different traditions. Benedict wanted his monks to listen carefully and reflect on what they had heard (RB 19.4,7). The emphasis was on careful selection of psalms in moderate quantities, clear reading and chanting, and participation through hymns, antiphons and the like.

A novice coming into the community would not have found this liturgy strange. Psalm singing had been popular among Christians of all social classes in the late fourth century;[89] this enthusiasm may have waned a little by Benedict's time, but it is likely that individuals still followed the advice of Jerome and others to 'rise at night for prayers and psalms'; and particular psalms, such as 50(51) and the evening psalm 140(141), had become so familiar that people probably incorporated them into their private devotions.[90]

---

88. RB 13.10. For discussions of Benedict's liturgy see Mitchell, 'Liturgical Code', pp.379-414; R. Taft, *The Liturgy of the Hours in East and West* (Collegeville: Liturgical Press, 1985), pp.130-40; Kardong, *Benedict's Rule*, pp.209-17.
89. J. McKinnon, *The Temple, the Church Fathers, and Early Western Chant* (Aldershot: Ashgate, 1998), article XI, 'Desert Monasticism and the Later Fourth-Century Psalmodic Movement'.
90. Taft, *Liturgy of the Hours*, p.143.

It was also common for lay people to pray at fixed hours during the day, as well as at sunrise and sunset. Monastic prayer may therefore have differed from that of the laity in intensity, but not greatly in content.

Lay Leadership within the Church

In the early centuries of Christianity, religious observance had been largely a private affair, carried on by families in their homes or shared with others in a community centre or one of the churches built within a villa complex by an aristocratic family head. The Church as an institution had not yet developed a parish system or built a sufficient number of public churches to accommodate all Christian worshippers. The church-building programme of the fifth century and the elaboration of the Church's organisation meant that, by the 490s, the pope and his officials were much more inclined to assert their authority over their powerful lay supporters.[91] Gelasius and Symmachus both exemplified this new trend.

The forthright attacks which Symmachus made on lay interference in church affairs may have been one of the reasons that inclined Benedict to support the Laurentians. Symmachus was, of course, taking a swipe at the large group of senators who had opposed his election. But behind his attack was a long-running struggle over the control of property donated to churches. Wealthy families were

91. For the church-building programme in Rome see R. Krautheimer, *Three Christian Capitals: Topography and Politics* (Berkeley and Los Angeles: University of California Press, 1983), pp.94-102.

trying to insist that donations made by their forebears should still be used as the donor had intended, whereas popes wanted to assert their right to sell, reinvest and generally manage property for the benefit of the Church as a whole. If Symmachus had sold donated property in order to pay election bribes – as was alleged – a sordid motivation was added to his breach of the donors' trust.

The issue revolved particularly around churches known as *tituli*, which had been founded or endowed by pious aristocrats and often still bore their benefactors' names. Bishops were partners in these foundations – indeed, in Rome some of the *tituli* building projects had been initiated by popes – but powerful lay donors inevitably felt a proprietorial concern for churches which were identified so closely with their families and their status in a particular neighbourhood. *Tituli* churches had quite a lengthy history, going back several generations and often commemorating a donor's relative who had been martyred in the days of persecution. They had their own liturgies, baptisteries and charitable programmes, and their priests ran their activities in conjunction with local families and benefactors, 'almost as self-sufficient microcosms of the Church'.[92]

Symmachus's attack seemed to threaten these long-established conventions of lay involvement in the running of the Church at the local level. It was no coincidence that at the

---

92. P.A.B. Llewellyn, 'The Roman church during the Laurentian schism: priests and senators', Church History, 45 (1976), p.420. Much has been written on the *tituli*; see especially K. Bowes, Private Worship, pp.65-71; A.H.M. Jones, 'Church Finance in the Fifth and Sixth Centuries', Journal of Theological Studies, 11 (1960), pp.84-94; and Sessa, Formation, pp.232-4. Julia Hillner, 'Families, patronage and the titular churches of Rome, 300-600', in K. Cooper and J. Hillner eds., Religion, Dynasty and Patronage in early Christian Rome, 300-900 (Cambridge University Press, 2007), pp.225-61 examines the legal position of the *tituli* and concludes that Symmachus had the law on his side. However, the issue was not primarily a legal one; it was Symmachus's challenge to local leadership, combined with his affront to custom and sentiment.

start of the schism many priests of the tituli churches backed Laurentius, himself a priest of the titulus Praxedis. It seems that they rallied increasingly to his side, for Laurentius was able to count on the loyalty of most churches in Rome from 502 until his forcible retirement in 506/7.

The tituli churches were only the most visible signs of a very broad tradition of family piety and household worship. This was the religious culture in which Benedict was born and grew up. In the days of persecution this had been the only kind of religious observance that Christians could safely practise; over the next two centuries, despite the gradual development of an institutional church, 'daily domestic prayer continued to be the seedbed of Christian daily life',[93] and in Benedict's lifetime, many forms of popular devotion continued as before. Most households kept up a rhythm of prayer from dawn to dusk; they observed rites, like lamp-lighting, and they venerated relics or shrines of family martyrs. Where possible, special rooms were set aside for worship and in due course a family of modest wealth, as Benedict's was, might incorporate a chapel in the layout of its house. In the fifth century, as more and more of the great senatorial families converted to Christianity, the modest house church grew in size and function and some acquired the status of tituli. The columned reception halls of aristocratic villas were converted into three-aisled, apsed basilicas, after the pattern of the new public churches of the city;[94] the liturgy grew in complexity and the congregation

---

93. Bowes, Private Worship, p.76. Bowes gives a detailed picture of religious life for the Christian laity and that forms the basis of the account given here. See also K. Bowes, 'Personal Devotions and Private Chapels' in V. Burrus ed., A People's History of Christianity, vol.2, Late Ancient Christianity (Minneapolis: Fortress Press, 2005), pp.188-210.
94. Some of the surviving churches from those days are described by H. Brandenburg, Ancient Churches of Rome from the Fourth to the Seventh Century: The Dawn of Christian Architecture in the West (Turnhout: Brepols, 2005), with excellent photographs and ground plans.

in size, as client families and neighbours were drawn in; and the new church might boast a complement of several priests and even a resident monk or two to act as teachers of scripture and spiritual guides.

Lay leadership also dominated the countryside, where landlords played a crucial role in spreading Christianity to the rural population, building churches, appointing priests and using their seigniorial influence to convert family members, servants and slaves.[95] Their country villas sometimes provided a home for experiments in lay asceticism, where couples lived a life of prayer and chastity or tended shrines to local saints.[96] In most cases these ascetic households made only modest alterations to their domestic routine because there was, during Benedict's lifetime, quite a strong current of disapproval of aristocratic families who forsook their traditional leadership roles and the wealth that gave them influence.

The involvement of families in the local life of the Church left bishops with a difficult balance to find: on the one hand, they wanted to encourage aristocratic involvement and charitable endowments, but on the other, they did not want the families to go too far as 'religious impresarios in their own right'.[97] This tension was very evident throughout Benedict's life, as centralising popes like Gelasius and Symmachus tried to control endowments and other religious practices.[98] In his property reforms of 502, Symmachus

---

95. Bowes, Private Worship, p.127. Christianisation 'cannot be understood without reference to the decisions of heads of households'; K. Cooper, 'Approaching the Holy Household', Journal of Early Christian Studies, 15 (2007), p. 137.
96. Sessa, Formation, pp.58-60 gives some examples and concludes: 'Monasticism was still very much a traditional domestic experience in late Roman Italy' (p.60).
97. Bowes, Private Worship, p.80.
98. Hillner, 'Families, patronage', pp. 251-2; Sessa, Formation, pp.162-73; J. Taylor, 'The Early Church at Work: Gelasius I (492-6)', Journal of Religious

agreed to accept some limitation on his right to manage donated property, but extended the same limitation to the priests of the tituli, a neat way of turning the tables on his opponents. Gelasius ruled that churches should not be consecrated by the local bishop without papal permission; in practice, consecration never seems to have been denied, which suggests that powerful landowners could build first and then lean on a bishop to perform the necessary ceremony. Estate owners had long been accustomed to appointing their own clergy. Early in the sixth century this was confirmed, with the proviso that the local bishop had to approve the appointment, but Pope Pelagius was still struggling in the 550s to get the proviso recognised in every case. Gelasius also ruled that his permission was needed to set up a martyr shrine. During the sixth century the names of family martyrs were gradually removed from tituli churches and replaced with more neutral dedications. The same desire to curb the growth of local centres of spiritual authority lay behind a ban on baptisteries in tituli and private churches. Instead, the Church wanted baptisms to be carried out in a bishop's church, so that the loyalties of new Christians would be focussed on the bishop.

Coming from a background of lay-clerical cooperation, Benedict may well have thought that Laurentius, with his experience of collaboration with the laity in the tituli, would have represented the Roman traditions of prayer and worship more sympathetically than Symmachus, the outsider and hard-line bureaucrat. Benedict would have regarded lay initiative and lay leadership as perfectly natural; he would have seen nothing at all incongruous in setting up a community of pious laymen seeking God together and following their own liturgy without clerical involvement.

History, 8 (1974-5), pp.317-32; S. Wood, The Proprietary Church in the Medieval West (Oxford University Press, 2006), pp.11-16; Brown, Eye of a Needle, pp.472-7.

In doing this, he was not repudiating the ecclesiastical establishment; indeed, he makes it clear in RB that a bishop might have a degree of authority over a monastic community.[99]

In fact, at this stage in the Church's history, the authority of bishops – and even of popes – was by no means well-defined or widely accepted and, in practice, some form of collaboration between clergy and laity had been the normal way of getting things done. We need to see Benedict's monasticism not just as descending from the earlier forms of monastic life in West and East, but as reflecting the character of Christian life at the local level in central Italy in the late-fifth and early-sixth century.

The Monastic Household

THE MOST IMPORTANT FORM of local leadership – in religious and ethical matters, as well as in the management of property and social relations – was the leadership of the household. The authority of the *dominus*, or head of the household, and the *paterfamilias*, or father of the family, created ripples of reciprocal obligation that reached into every corner of life, especially as the two roles were usually united in one person.[100]

---

99. RB 62.9 and 64.4. In 64.4 Benedict goes on to say that 'Christians in the area' might also dismiss and replace an unworthy abbot. This was the kind of initiative that the aristocracy might have taken in the *tituli* and house churches of Rome.

100. See R.P. Saller, '*Pater familias, mater familias*, and the Gendered Semantics of the Roman Household', *Classical Philology*, 94 (1999), pp.182-97. Saller says that the term *pater familias* was used mainly in legal contexts, where

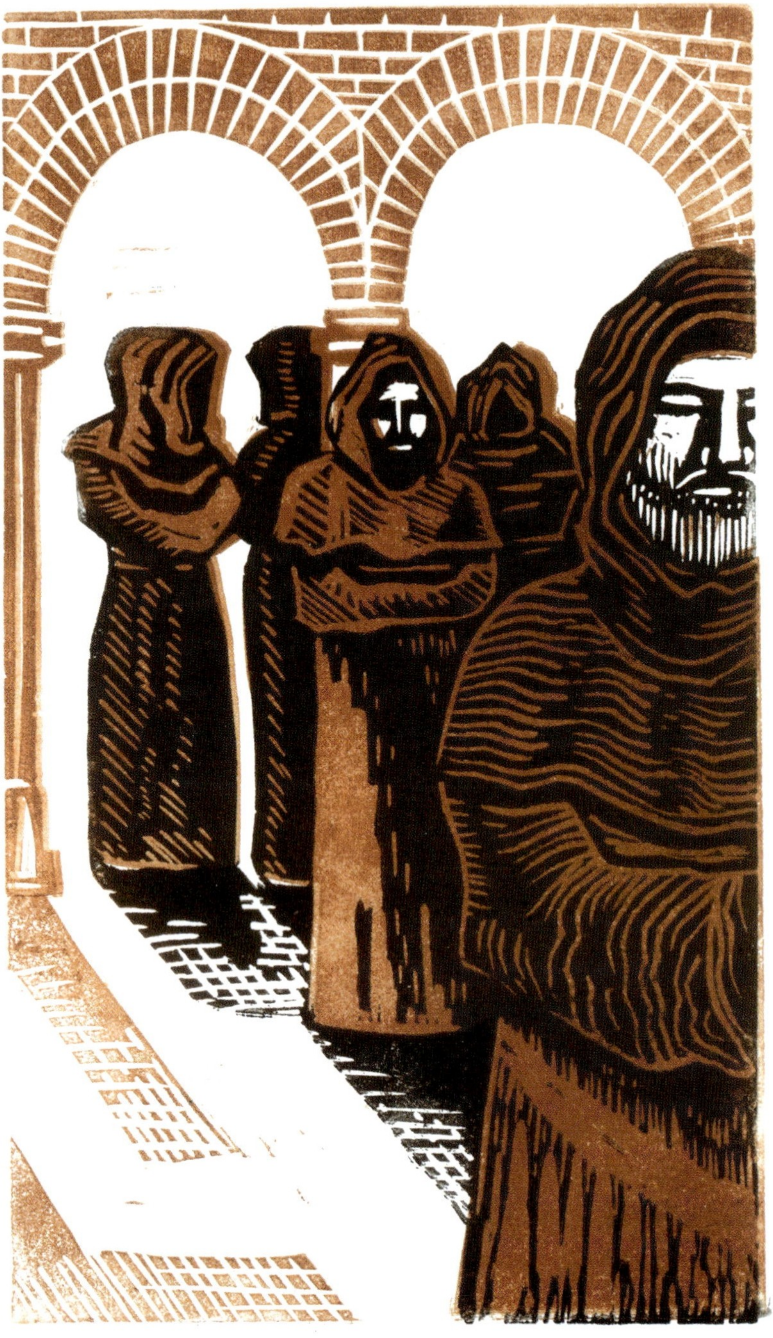

Benedict says that the abbot of a monastery should be called *dominus et abbas* (RB 63.13). In using the word *abba* for 'father', Benedict pointed his monks towards the tradition of the Desert Fathers and, beyond that, to the New Testament (e.g. RB 2.3).

The word *dominus*, on the other hand, would have had a very contemporary resonance for his community. Everyone would have connected it immediately with the role of the household head in the society all around them, and in which they had grown up.[101] In theory, the *dominus* had extremely autocratic powers over persons and property within his household and estate and many of those same powers can be seen in the role that Benedict prescribes for the abbot of a monastery.[102] Both the household head and the abbot could expect 'unhesitating obedience' (RB 5.1) and could enforce

'it provided a concept that organised much of Roman law about property rights' (p.188); 'the most common meaning of *pater familias* in all extant, classical, nonlegal texts is "estate owner", without reference to family relations' (p.190).

101. Kardong (*Benedict's Rule*, p.66) condemns all socio-political interpretations of the abbot's role, insisting that Benedict's only source was scriptural. Unfortunately, this involves Kardong in inconsistency, for when it comes to other matters – such as corporal punishment – he falls back upon the customs of 'ancient times' as an explanation (p.59). Kardong particularly condemns the implications that have been drawn from the word *paterfamilias*. However, the important word in this context is *dominus*. Kardong says merely that *dominus* was the word 'used in ordinary parlance to adddress a powerful man' (p.521) when, in fact, it had a particular connotation that was loaded with social significance for Benedict and his contemporaries. *Dominus* is also used by Benedict to refer to the Lord Christ, but Benedict is happy to allow this ambiguity to persist as it supports his contention that the abbot 'holds the place of Christ' in the monastery (RB 63.13).

102. The following comparison owes much to O. Norderval, 'The Benedictine Transformation of Roman Villa Life', *Acta ad Archaeologiam et Artium Historiam Pertinenta*, 16 (2002), pp.31-38. But Norderval lacks the nuanced understanding of Roman society found in, for example, R.P. Saller, *Patriarchy, Property and Death in the Roman Family* (Cambridge University Press, 1994). See also K. Cooper, 'Approaching the Holy Household' and K. Cooper, *The Fall of the Roman Household* (Cambridge University Press, 2007).

this with a range of punishments, from whipping (RB 23.5, 71.9) to expulsion from the community (RB 28.6). The *paterfamilias* originally had powers of life and death over members of a Roman household, though these powers were very seldom used; Benedict would hardly have wanted to reproduce them, but an echo can be seen in his statement that, after entering the monastery, a monk 'will not have even his own body at his disposal' (RB 58.25). Similar powers applied to property. The *dominus* owned and controlled all property belonging to the household or created by its members; likewise, the abbot expected his monks to give up all their possessions when they entered the monastery (RB 58.24 and 59.3) and to depend on the abbot for clothing and anything else they might need (RB 33.1-5 and 55.17-19).

In practice, the powers of the *paterfamilias* were circumscribed in all sorts of ways, so that the reality of life in the household was very different from the legal stereotype. One brake on autocracy was the *consilium* or council of close family members. The *paterfamilias* was not obliged to take its advice, but he might not get legal backing for his actions if he did not consult it.[103] Benedict made similar provision for discussion in the monastery (RB 3), using the same term – *consilium* – to describe it; this involved the whole community in important matters, otherwise the seniors only. The abbot was to ponder the brothers' advice, but the final decision was his alone (RB 3.5). He was urged to listen carefully, even to the most junior members of the community (RB 3.3), and to make proper allowance for the character and intelligence of each individual (RB 2.32).

The *consilium* must have been a major influence on Benedict as he grew into his own role as abbot. The governance of his community in the early stages must have

---

103. S. Dixon, *The Roman Family* (Baltimore and London: 1992), pp. 27, 47, 159; W.K. Lacey, '*Patria Potestas*' in B. Rawson ed., *The Family in Ancient Rome: New Perspectives* (London: Routledge, 1992), pp.137-40.

been a process of improvisation and experiment arising from Benedict's own strongly-held convictions, followed by discussion with the monks and the reaching of a consensus. That consensus clearly owed much to the monks' inherited beliefs about Roman social norms. It was probably only later, as the community grew in size and its management in complexity, that Benedict looked about for written Rules to see how other abbots had dealt with similar situations.

In practice, the severity of the Roman *paterfamilias* seldom, if ever, came close to the traditional stereotype; authority was often softened by love and indulgence. Roman homilies on the behaviour of parents and estate owners recommended 'dutiful and gentle affection of parents towards children'[104] and a combination of affection and justice in dealings with slaves. Filial piety, the conventional response to parental authority, was also a complex pattern of behaviour; instead of mere obedience and submission it often demonstrated real love and respect for parents and 'a more broadly affectionate devotion among all family members'.[105] Benedict picked up these nuances in his discussion of the relationship between abbot and monks. Monks ought to show 'unfeigned and humble love' to their abbot (RB 72.10) and to their fellow monks 'the pure love of brothers' (RB 72.8), showing mutual obedience (RB 71) and 'supporting with the greatest patience one another's weaknesses of body or behaviour' (RB 72.5). The abbot ought 'to show equal love to everyone' (RB 2.22); where appropriate be 'devoted and tender as only a father can be' (RB 2.24); 'be discerning and moderate' (RB 64.17); and 'strive to be loved rather than feared' (RB 64.15). Above all, the abbot had to remember that 'the shepherd will bear

---

104. Valerius Maximus, *Memorable Doings and Sayings* ed. and trans. D.R. Shackleton Bailey for Loeb Classical Library (Harvard University Press, 2000), 5.7. This and other literary sources are discussed by Saller, *Patriarchy*, pp.108-110.
105. Saller, *Patriarchy*, p.131.

the blame wherever the father of the household finds that the sheep have yielded no profit' (RB 2.7), that he must show his flock 'all that is good and holy more by example than by words' (RB 2.12) and that 'on judgment day he will surely have to submit a reckoning to the Lord for all their souls – and indeed for his own as well'. (RB 2.38).

This broad responsibility for the spiritual welfare of all one's dependents was part of the traditional role of the household head. It continued in Benedict's time and was expressed in the homilies written for wealthy householders who were managing large estates. For example, Gregoria, a female landowner of the early sixth century, was urged to 'be a model for all your servants'; 'let them see your eyes continually lifted to the heavens . . . By this model you will secure your own salvation and that of those over whom you have been worthy to rule'.[106] Presumably Benedict did not see that text, which was private to Gregoria, but he would have been aware of debate about the proper role of landowners, a topic that had been discussed in public over the previous century. Pope Leo I had preached on the subject and other homilies on leadership, such as the one written for Demetrias, a member of the powerful family of Anicii, could well have circulated among the elite.[107] Some of the particular precepts in these homilies are paralleled in RB: for example, the dangers of back-biting and murmuring, or using the force of habit to make the whole of life virtuous (cf. RB 7.68). However, the homilies are mainly concerned to make

---

106. *Ad Gregoriam in palatio*, 18. This text is discussed throughout Cooper, *Fall*, and a full translation is provided in an appendix. The homily is thought to have been written during the reign of Theodoric.

107. The Anicii homily was the *Epistola ad Demetriadem de vera humilitate*, thought to have been written about 440, possibly by Pope Leo, but more probably by Prosper of Aquitaine. Demetrias had been a nun, but renounced the veil in order to take up the management of some of the family estates. See also the homily preserved in a Bobbio mss. discussed by Cooper, *Fall*, pp.119-22.

a general point: that there are essential spiritual benefits to be gained from an ordered and well-balanced community life. As the letter to Demetrias put it: when seekers after truth 'sever themselves from the love of things temporal . . . they experience an increase in sensibility, not a decrease; instead of losing vigour of mind, they receive the light of extraordinary understanding. They live in this world, but they detach themselves from the tumult of the world'.[108] The Roman ethical tradition, now strongly influenced by Christianity, ran parallel with the specifically Christian tradition that Benedict learnt from the scriptures and the Church Fathers. What proportion of Benedict's spirituality was derived from each of these sources it is impossible to say, but it seems clear that RB is based, in part, upon the inherited culture of its author and is not simply developed from Benedict's reading of Christian texts or borrowed from earlier monastic Rules.

THE MONASTERY IN THE WORLD

IN THE EARLY SIXTH CENTURY most monasteries in Italy were small, poor and suburban, or pushed out to marginal lands where the major source of subsistence was likely to have been the herding of animals.[109]

Benedict's community was different in every respect. It was large enough, first to outgrow its original home in Subiaco, and then to send a detachment of monks from

108. *Epistola ad Demetriam*, 4, quoted in A. Kurdock, 'Demetrias ancilla dei: Anicia Demetrias and the problem of the missing patron' in Cooper and Hillner, *Religion, Dynasty and Patronage*, p. 218.
109. Brown, *Rise of Western Christendom*, pp. 221-2.

Monte Cassino to found a new monastery at Terracina (D 22.1) It attracted the support of wealthy patrons; indeed, the various stages of expansion would hardly have been possible without them—for example, the cost of carrying a large quantity of building materials to the top of Monte Cassino must have been considerable.[110] Aristocratic families who moved to Constantinople often donated their estates to the Church and it seems reasonable to assume that Benedict's community benefited in the same way. Much of the donated land must have been good quality arable, capable of producing crops of wheat; a mill is listed in RB as one of the monastery's outbuildings and, if the *Dialogue* is to be believed, a sickle was a valuable item, since a monk who lost one was conscious of committing a serious offence.[111]

Benedict told his monks not to be distracted by talk of the world outside the monastery, but Benedict himself must have been worried very often by worldly business. It seems reasonable to suppose that, while a small community might have lived from hand to mouth on cash donations, a larger one would have needed a steadier and more reliable income stream from land and other investments.[112] An abbot was necessarily a financial administrator and manager of the monastery's involvement in local markets. It is clear

---

110. There are several references in the *Dialogue* to the community's aristocratic connections, e.g. D 3.14; 17.1; 22.1. Some idea of the cost and labour of building a monastery for about 30 monks can be gained from a report on the excavation of the abbey at Alatri, which was built in the 520s. Benedict and his monks are said to have rested there on their journey from Subiaco to Monte Cassino. Alatri's abbey church was about the same size and shape as Monte Cassino's. E. Fentress and C.J. Goodson, 'Patricians, Monks and Nuns: the Abbey of S. Sebastiano, Alatri during the Middle Ages', *Archeologia Medievale*, 30 (2003), pp.67-105.
111. RB 66.6; D 6.1-2.
112. This is suggested by B. Brenk, 'Monasteries as rural settlements: patron-dependence or self-sufficiency?' in W. Bowden, L. Lavan and C. Machado eds., *Recent Research on the Late Antique Countryside* (Leiden: Brill, 2003), pp.453-55.

that the monastery's fields were normally cultivated by hired labourers or tenants (RB 48.7); these had to be supervised, either directly or through agents. Agents would have been used to supervise the monastery's more distant endowments, which would have passed into the community's possession with a population of tenants and tied labourers of various kinds, including slaves. Agents and tenants had to be given instructions and, perhaps, occasionally inspected.

Oversight of the monastic economy must have become more and more problematic in the last decades of Benedict's life. Agriculture would have been disrupted by passing armies. Demand for agricultural products from Campania would have shrunk as the market in Rome contracted with the city's declining population. The situation may have been exacerbated by the pandemic of the 540s, which could have caused a shortage of agricultural labour and a rise in the costs of production.[113] Not that these pressures were a misfortune for everyone; in the south of Italy, particularly, new crops and new groups of landowners arose to take the place of those that had disappeared. Either way, a greater burden of management would have fallen upon the abbot and his agents as they tried to adapt to these changes.

Providing leadership of this kind was one of the traditional duties of the *dominus*. However, when writing about the abbot in this role (RB 64.5), Benedict uses a much more managerial term – *dispensator* – which Romans understood as steward or treasurer. In doing this Benedict was probably trying to emphasise the importance of the

---

113. The impact of plague on population cannot be quantified, but it seems that there was a general decline in population in the 5th-7th centuries and a long-term decline in rural prosperity in central and southern Italy. B. Ward-Perkins, 'Land, labour and settlement' and 'Specialized production and exchange' in *Cambridge Ancient History*, vol. XIV, pp.323 and 355.

abbot's economic activities.[114] But another significant motive would have been to situate the abbot and his community within the contemporary debate about stewardship. During the fifth century there had been increasing emphasis on the responsibilities of the wealthy to administer their possessions as a kind of stewardship for their households, for society more widely, for the poor especially, and for the Church. It was argued by Pope Leo and others that God was the ultimate *dominus* and the aristocratic landowner was merely a steward on God's behalf. If this represented, in some respects, a curb on the landowner's power to do what he liked with his property, it represented an increase in his authority as a spiritual leader guiding his household to a heavenly home. The concept of stewardship provided 'a middle ground between extreme ideals of ascetic renunciation and traditional norms of domesticity'[115] and was therefore an answer to those who feared that Christian landowners might be withdrawing from their social duty. Benedict saw the running of the monastery as a form of stewardship, with the abbot having both a dominant role in the community and yet having to give an account of his actions to God (RB 64.21; see also 53.22). At the same time Benedict was reassuring critics of monasticism that his monastery was a stable and well-ordered community in the world—God's world.

The uncertain outlook for agriculture may have prompted Benedict to follow the example of other monasteries and diversify the community's economy into handicraft production. The monastic workshop recently excavated at the Crypta Balbi in Rome was, in Benedict's lifetime, producing a range of goods in metal, bone and glass to cater both for pilgrims and for the more expensive tastes of the

---

114. Brenk notes Benedict's use of economic terminology in various parts of RB; 'Monasteries as rural settlements', p.455.
115. Sessa, *Formation*, p.83.

city's elite.[116] Benedict may have hoped for – and needed – similar developments at Monte Cassino. This would account for the chapter in RB on artisans (RB 57), which is otherwise rather surprising in a Rule that generally emphasises the separation of the monastery from the world. Some of the artisan-monks were expected to produce goods of high quality (RB 57.2), indicating a fashionable clientele, though the 'various crafts' mentioned in a later chapter (RB 66.6) are more hum-drum. Benedict warns against any spirit of commercialism or pride in craftsmanship for its own sake; artisans must work humbly, avoid avarice and fraud in their dealings with the secular world and allow local craftsmen to take the major share of the market.[117]

It may be that the need to diversify the monastery's sources of income was one of the reasons for the move from Subiaco to Monte Cassino. Subiaco was a backwater, not a place for picking up passing trade. Monte Cassino, on the other hand, was adjacent to a major highway. The markets and hostelries in the town at the foot of the mountain would have done a brisk business with people travelling between Rome and the south and the monks would have found a good outlet there for the products of the monastic workshops and gardens.

The porter was a pivotal figure in the monastery's economic relations with the outside world. It is easy to see why Benedict attached so much importance to his appointment. He needed to be a 'sensible old man' (RB 66.1), unfailingly courteous but a shrewd judge of character. He needed to understand the whole business of the monastery,

116. F. Dell'Acqua, 'Craft production in early western monasticism; rules, spaces, products' in H. Dey and E. Fentress eds., *Western Monasticism ante Literam; The Spaces of Monastic Observance in Late Antiquity and the Early Middle Ages* (Turnhout: Brepols, 2011), pp.297-8.
117. This, and the undesirable consequences of being sucked into a world of commercial calculation, seem to have been behind Benedict's rather curious (and possibly counter-productive) instructions on pricing goods below the local rate (RB 57.8).

know which monks needed to receive visitors or messages, judge which dealers and middlemen to admit and which to turn politely away, and know how all this could be done without disrupting the calm and order of the community as a whole. This was no job for a novice.

Benedict seems to have guided his community safely through the last decades of Ostrogothic rule, but monks elsewhere fell on hard times. Some communities may have been driven out of their monasteries by war or the drying up of their endowments; others who had lived in ones and twos in wealthy households might have found themselves homeless as their aristocratic patrons fell into poverty or decamped to the East. Many of them must have taken to the road and turned up at Monte Cassino looking for shelter—and also genuinely looking for membership of another monastic community. These must be the visiting monks that Benedict writes about in RB 61, monks with a real commitment to their vocation and a valuable experience of it in other monasteries. Benedict outlines a process for accepting them as permanent members of the community, but adds that the abbot should always seek permission from the visitor's former abbot, if he was known – or if he could be traced.[118] These visitors would not have been confused with the perpetually wandering monks – the so-called sarabaites and gyrovagues – who were viewed so disapprovingly by Benedict (RB 1.6-11) because of their lack of principles and their beggarly way of life. An experienced porter would easily have recognised those scavengers of the monastic life and given them short shrift.

118. RB 61 makes perfectly good sense on the assumption that Benedict was writing about displaced or refugee monks. Otherwise, the chapter seems self-contradictory, with Benedict first encouraging, and then condemning, the 'poaching' of monks from other communities. Some of the visitors may have been monk-priests, which explains why Benedict places this chapter between the two chapters on the position of priests in the monastery.

Conclusion

THE CONTEXT MOST USUALLY GIVEN for RB is a comparison with the *Rule of the Master*, a monastic Rule which is usually thought to have been written in the vicinity of Rome about thirty years before Benedict wrote RB.[119] Useful though the comparison has been in showing Benedict's priorities, this approach has left the two Rules floating together above the surface of history, detached from events. Benedict needs a clearer historical context. In any case, the history of monasticism needs to be more than the history of monastic Rules.

Benedict's whole life was lived under the influence of three long-term developments: the relationship between the Goths and the Italo-Romans, which was overtaken by war; the steady growth in the centralised power of the Church in Rome; and the theological conflict between Rome and the provinces of the East.

Once Theodoric had settled on to his throne, relations between Goths and Romans were relatively unproblematic, as was the relationship between Arianism and Catholicism. Benedict, too, is unlikely to have been troubled by the Goths or by their Arian beliefs. After Theodoric had died and Justinian had launched his war of reconquest, the political

---

119. Agreement about this is not quite unanimous. For opposing views see M. Dunn, 'Mastering Benedict: monastic rules and their authors in the early medieval West', *English Historical Review*, 105 (1990), pp.567-94 and A. de Vogüé, 'The Master and St Benedict: a reply to Marilyn Dunn', EHR, 107 (1992), pp.95-103 with a rejoinder by Dunn, pp.104-11. See also M. Dunn, *The Emergence of Monasticism: from the Desert Fathers to the Early Middle Ages* (Oxford: Blackwell, 2003).

situation became more fluid and more dangerous. Benedict was clearly dismayed by the war and did his best to mitigate its effects on the people living around the monastery (D 21.1-2, 28.1-2). Benedict was probably also alert to the military and geo-political changes taking place around the Mediterranean through the impact that these had on the wealth of his aristocratic supporters. During the first half of the sixth century, many elite families found themselves in straitened circumstances and were forced to divest themselves of their remaining lands, either selling them or donating them to the Church.

By the end of the sixth century the Church had grown enormously in power. It was the largest landowner in Italy and the wealthiest institution, and its bishops were often the leading political figures in their cities, with a social status to match. At the same time the Church had codified and elaborated its canon law, enlarged its central secretariat, taken on more charitable activities and taken over more churches and shrines. For most of the fifth century, the Church had had to strike a balance between its ambitions and its need to rely on aristocratic patronage. From about 480, the year of Benedict's birth, the balance began to tip decisively in the Church's favour. Benedict's monastic community can be seen as an attempt to conserve what was best in the old forms of lay piety and lay leadership, now wilting under the Church's institutional power.

Rome's control over doctrine, however, was much more difficult to achieve, as can be seen very clearly in the long struggle with the East: with monophysite theologians, emperors, patriarchs and angry congregations. Successive eruptions of controversy – over the Henotikon, Theopaschism and the Three Chapters – kept the issue alive throughout Benedict's life. This aspect of Benedict's milieu has been ignored by commentators, but it is most unlikely that Benedict himself was able to ignore it. The few hints available in RB suggest that Benedict took an irenic approach to theology, looking for common ground and reconciliation.

When theological and institutional issues combined, as they did in the schism of 498-506, it seems likely that Benedict preferred the stance of those who favoured theological moderation and the traditional patterns of lay-clerical cooperation.

RB is not a work of theology; it is a manual of practice, the prospectus of 'a school for the Lord's service' (RB Prol.45). Nevertheless, it is soaked in Benedict's understanding of the scriptures and conditioned by the theology of his day. It is easy to overlook Benedict's accomplishment in completing RB in a form that has stood the test of centuries of study and practice. The modern commentator comes to RB with the same authors that Benedict knew, but in vastly greater quantities. In the case of Augustine, for example, it is very likely that Benedict first became acquainted with Augustine's ideas at second hand, from discussions in the household or the academy and from the general culture of the time, and then from reading some of the *florilegia* of extracts; only later would he have read any of Augustine's works in their entirety, and perhaps only a limited number of those. Benedict's first experience of biblical exegesis may have been the *cento* of Proba. Books of that kind and the classical literature of his student days would not necessarily have blunted Benedict's appreciation of Christian texts; on the contrary, they may have sharpened it and encouraged an approach that was both analytical and eclectic. In RB Benedict has distilled all these influences into a text that is fresh, accessible and firmly biblical.

Benedict may seem a rather conservative character, with his fondness for traditional household structures and traditional household piety. But in other respects he was radical for his time. Household heads were not elected, as the abbot was. The egalitarianism of the monastery was an extraordinary break with the conventions of late Roman society. Novice monks exchanged a society that was stratified by wealth and birth for a community where they were ranked according to the order in which they had joined (RB 63.1,7). Some of them clearly found it difficult to get accustomed to this new situation (D 20.1-2). Over everything stood the RB. If the monastery was an island of stability as armies marched by and society was thrown into confusion, RB was the point of entry to a more profound stability, a stability greater than anything then offered by the Church, with its theological controversies and the ever-expanding complexities of its canon law. Benedict offered the monk a stability of heart and mind in the service of Christ.

RB did not preclude all change, especially the change required for spiritual growth. It was, said Benedict modestly, only a rule 'for beginners' and 'loftier summits' lay beyond (RB 73.8-9). But Benedict might have been surprised at some of the changes that took place in the following centuries, such as the widespread clericalisation of monastic communities. Benedictine monasticism has been seen as the beginning of a new religious phase, characteristic of medieval Europe, in which monks were clearly distinguished from the laity by their cowls and tonsures and by their dedication to an ascetic regime in expiation of their sins.[120] These traits may have been present in Benedict's community in embryonic form but their full development belonged to later generations. Benedict prescribed cowls and tunics for his monks and implied that these should be uniform across the community and distinct from the clothing of the laity—but not so distinct that they could not vary in colour and quality 'according to local conditions and climate' (RB 55.1-7).[121]

120. Brown, *Rise of Western Christendom*, pp. 223-25.
121. Benedict appears to be following Cassian, who says that monks' clothing 'should be different from the apparel of this world', consisting

RB does, of course, refer to sin and the need for contrition, compunction and conversion of life. But grinding mortification is not part of Benedict's thinking; indeed, he goes out of his way to promise 'nothing harsh, nothing burdensome' (RB Prol.46). The tone of RB is one of promise rather than of penance; he tells his monks that 'we shall run on the path of God's commandments, our hearts overflowing with the inexpressible delight of love' (RB Prol.49). Benedict was not a medieval figure. He comes to us from the context of an earlier age, but is not contained by it.

---

not in 'strangeness . . . but in decent simplicity'. Institutes, 1: ii and x. The wearing of a tonsure was gradually becoming a sign of the monastic calling, but Benedict does not prescribe it in RB and was unhappy at the way that sarabaites flaunted this custom (RB 1.7).

About the Author

RICHARD NEWMAN is a former university lecturer who has published research on the histories of India, China and New Zealand. He is a Fellow of the Royal Historical Society. He is now retired and lives in the south of England, where he is an oblate of a Benedictine community.